The
New
Romans

The
New
Romans

Candid Canadian Opinions of the U.S.

edited by
A. W. Purdy

St. Martin's Press
NEW YORK

First published in the United States of America in 1968
by St. Martin's Press, Inc., 175 Fifth Avenue,
New York, N.Y. 10010

Library of Congress Catalog Card number 68-55579

Printed in Canada and bound in the United States of
America

Contents

Contents

Acknowledgements

The Tamarack Review for "Cape Breton Is the Thought Control Center of Canada," by Ray Smith. This story was shortened by the editor for publication here.

The Village Voice, The Spectator, and *Archives Diplomatiques et Consulaires* for "If Throughout His Reign Napoleon . . .," by Stephen Vizinczey.

House of Anansi for "The Generation of Hunters," by Dave Godfrey.

McClelland & Stewart Ltd. for "Billboards Build Freedom of Choice," by Earle Birney.

Atlas for "O Canada," by Louis Dudek.

The Open Letter and *20 Cents Magazine* for "Winning," by George Bowering.

Canadian Dimension for "Centennial Song," by Robin Mathews.

All other contributions were especially written for *The New Romans.*

The articles by Naim Kattan and André Major were translated from the French by Joyce Marshall.

A. W. P.

The New Romans

Introduction

A. W. Purdy

The idea for this book was the brainchild of Mel Hurtig and myself in Edmonton early in 1967. We intended it to be a book unlike any other previously published. Other books have discussed trade and diplomatic relations and the various territorial "adjustments" of the lamentably undefended American-Canadian border. Most of these are phrased in language that might cause the reader to think a corporate merger was being discussed between Coca-Cola and Carling's Brewery. No book has appeared (at least to my knowledge) that describes frankly how Canadians feel about the United States.

We envisioned a book that would say, in absolutely biased terms, how many Canadian writers — and it follows, many other Canadians too — feel about the U.S. and Americans. Do we really *like* Americans as individuals and as a people? Do Canadians feel that the U.S. is pursuing a just and honourable policy with its military presence in Southeast Asia? Considering the U.S. as the ranking world power, do Canadians feel that the U.S. is using that power badly or that it does more harm than good in the world today?

These are hard and hurtful questions, and even to ask them may seem somehow nasty and hitting below the belt — to some people.

Above all we wanted the book to express both emotional and soundly logical attitudes. But whether the writers actually wrote their contributions with that type of content in mind was entirely up to them, just as the responsibility for the book's title belongs to the publisher and myself. As it turned out, in most cases the writers did express emotional attitudes — some of which I agree with, some of which I do not.

Both the publisher and I reject the "glass house" type of thinking which maintains that Canadians should not throw stones at the U.S. because our own country is also vulnerable and has many serious problems which we have not been able to solve thus far in our existence as a nation. And many Canadians do feel that we, as Canadians, should mind our own business, "cultivate our garden," and keep our mouths shut about other people.

To these I would reply that the most powerful nation on earth is everyone's business, for what happens in the U.S. affects every Canadian. We believe that no one, no individual and no nation, should be immune to critical examination and discussion. One could easily say that no one is perfect, but some of us are less perfect. Yet it is not from a "holier than thou" viewpoint that we examine our attitudes towards the U.S. and try to resolve our often ambiguous feelings about that country.

Canada has an Indian problem of growing seriousness; it suffers poverty and underdevelopment in many areas. We are also faced with the danger of Canada's being split into two parts by the withdrawal from Confederation of one of its two founding peoples.

But those are internal difficulties, which are of most concern to Canada alone. At this time they do not affect the rest of the world (except possibly Charles de Gaulle), as does the presence of the U.S. in Asia, as does the interracial violence in the U.S., along with that other personal violence which seems to be a national characteristic of Americans. All of these are a threat to international equilibrium.

With all this in mind as possible subject matter (but not mentioned to contributors), writers were asked to reveal how they felt about the U.S. and Americans — from their personal viewpoint — concerning any aspect of the subject. They were asked to say whatever they wanted to say, whether flattering or unflattering to the U.S., and to keep it relatively brief so that as many opinions as possible could be included in the proposed book.

One thing I have noticed from reading the articles in this collection: most Canadians cannot talk about the U.S. outside the context of themselves as Canadians. That they discuss everything from this particular viewpoint really shouldn't surprise me. Yet after having demonstrated possession of a Canadian viewpoint, many of them would deny that they know what being a Canadian consists of — ! And as a passing comment, there are few things I find more irritating about my own country than this so-called "search for an identity," an identity which I've never doubted having in the first place.

The environment, the land, the people, and the flux of history have made us what we are; these have existed since Canada's beginning, along with a capacity for slow evolvement into something else that goes on and on. And perhaps I would also include pride. Their total is all that any nation may possess. I think it is enough.

Some writers are not included who should have been; we did ask them. I regret that there are not more Quebec writers represented here. Approximately fifteen were asked to contribute. I do not know whether their relative absence reflects a lack of concern on the part of Quebec writers or their greater concern with the problems of Quebec. In any case, I regret their absence.

The principle determining final selection of these articles and poems was literary merit — i.e., I asked myself the question: is this article or poem interesting? Whatever my own feelings about the United States, I would not reject a pro-American article or poem for this book — *if* it were well written.

There are some areas this book does not cover; for instance, the anti-war attitude of American intellectuals — James Dickey and John dos Passos are the only "hawks" I can think of among these. I cannot conceive of the open opposition to government that exists in the U.S. regarding the Vietnam War happening in very many countries. And I would like to have seen U.S. intervention in the affairs of South American countries dealt with separately, instead of being mentioned only in passing by contributors.

These are defects in the method used to compile this book, if they are defects at all. Apart from articles or poems taken from outside sources, writers were asked to choose whatever aspect of the subject they wished, and this they have done. The result is a book that reveals Canadian emotions and biases towards the U.S. in a way no other book even attempts. It spells out our feelings, involvements, shortcomings, and neuroses as a nation, and I think it is honest about them.

Some of the opinions in this book are strong meat for a public accustomed to hasty disavowals of anti-Americanism on the part of our politicians and daily newspapers. But if these opinions are controversial and have the effect of starting a dialogue on, say, fair and adequate taxation of American branch plants, then it may be earlier than the pessimists think, and Canadian sovereignty might become more than a vote-getting delusion for politicians.

I happen to think it is *already* too late. Therefore, all this book may do is register a sullen protest, a belated yap from a captive dog. It will scarcely raise more than an eyebrow on the big real estate dealers in Ottawa who have sold this country down the river to the Americans for the last thirty years. In fact, I think the book will be amusing to those citizens of a second-class nation who are unable to comprehend their own subservience or their own naive stupidity. But for some Canadians the book will not be amusing.

Letter to My Son

Farley Mowat

My dear Sandy:

A couple of months ago you asked me whether I thought it had been worthwhile to have spent so much of my time and energy tilting against American windmills. Feeling that there was a certain measure of condescension in the question, I replied with one of my facile, TV-type answers: to wit, that there can be no other real choice open to a Canadian except to resist the Yanks and all their works so that we, as a people and a nation, may escape being ingested into the Eagle's gut, never to emerge again except — maybe — as a patch of excrement upon the pages of world history.

That should have disposed of your question — but it didn't, and the damned thing has been festering within me ever since. It has finally forced me, very reluctantly you can believe, to make a new evaluation of the belief which has sustained me through some twenty years of waging verbal warfare against the encroachments of Uncle Sam. Have I indeed been wasting my time? I'm afraid, God help me, that I have. I can no longer convince myself that we have even a snowball's chance in hell of escaping ultimate ravishment at the hands of the Yankee succubus. And what really hurts is the belated recognition on my part that there never *was* much chance; that Canadians have become so fatally infected with a compulsive desire to be screwed, blued, and tatooed as minions of the U.S.A. that they not only do not wish to be saved — they are willing to fight against salvation with all the ferocity of cornered rats.

So wipe that smug smile off your face. You knew it all along, eh? Well, I should have known it too. God wot, enough people have tried to put me straight. There was Joey Small-

1

wood for one (as smart a promoter as ever hustled a vote), who gave me a fatherly lecture about a year ago. "What the U.S. wants, it will get," he told me. "And if we don't *give* them what they want, they'll take it anyway. And what they want — is most of what we've got."

That was about as clear an expression of *Realpolitik* as one can expect from the political animal, even if it was primarily a rationalization intended to excuse our political masters for having *already* given the Yanks almost everything of any value in this country. Nevertheless, Joey's point was well taken since those who rule us (they do not "govern" — that word implies statesmanship combined with honourable intentions) have, for their own reasons, long since sold us out. Or maybe they just saw the light a long way back and, in keeping with their dubious professional practices, took the line of least resistance. Some of them, that is. Others sold out with deliberate intent. One day I must tell you the full and stirring story of one of the greatest of all such salesmen — C. D. Howe — and of how *he* put us on the block. Of course, Howe's plan was to sell us down the river on the national scale, and we've progressed since then. Now every single province is trying to conduct its own sellout, in direct competition with the Ottawa salesmen, and it wouldn't surprise me much to see the game, which is called "who'll sell out the mostest, the soonest," reach right down to the municipal level before too long. Hell, what am I saying? It is past that point already. Witness the almost frantic rush of businessmen and owners of Canadian resources to sell themselves and their holdings ("*their* holdings"? I mean *ours*, of course) for a quick handful of Yankee bucks.

Joey wasn't the only one to point me in the direction of acute awareness, and I must add, in my own defense, that I wasn't as stupid as you may think. I realized what the politicians, at least, were up to ages ago. My naivety — if such it was — lay in my continuing conviction that the *people* of this land would not forever continue to acquiesce in this piecemeal betrayal of themselves and of their country. I was much influenced by what took place in Cuba and, before that, in Mexico. I believed that if such small, relatively powerless serf states could muster the guts to really kick Big Uncle in the backside, the people of Canada might be goaded into an equivalent demonstration of courage. Alas, Canadians are not Mexicans or Cubans, and I realize now that I miscalculated on a horrendous scale in ever thinking that Canadians would risk cutting off rich Uncle's dole by assuming the posture of a Man.

This is a fact that I am going to have to learn to live with. We have become a ·prostrate people — by our own volition. Actually the only time Canadians even raise themselves on their elbows these days is to *defend* their chosen masters and to attack, with the bitter hostility only known to turncoats, those who dare reproach them for their spineless espousal of slave status. (If this letter to you should ever see publication, the response in the "Letters To The Editor" column will show you what I mean!)

But there is no point in running on about what's past. My concern is for the future, because the future contains the world in which you'll have to live. So I have a few words of wisdom for you. Here speaks the hoary elder, and if I belabour the obvious a bit, bear with me.

Despite poor old Lester Pearson's recent statement in *Maclean's* that "the Americans are the least imperialistic people in history" (honest to God — that's what he said!), the Yanks now control the largest empire the world has ever known. Its citizens have, as Henry R. Luce (founder of Canada's two favourite magazines — *Life* and *Time*) once put it, now risen to the challenge: "to accept wholeheartedly the duty and opportunity as the most powerful and vital nation in the world and in consequence to exert upon the world the full impact of our influence, *for such purposes as we see fit and by such means as we see fit*" (italics mine). In this delightfully frank statement, combined with one by John Foster Dulles — "There are two ways of conquering a foreign nation. One is to gain control of its people by force of arms. The other is to gain control of its economy by financial means." — you have the essential dogma subscribed to by the military-political-economic hegemony that runs the U.S.A. Once you understand this dogma you will have no difficulty understanding the true significance of current events in Spain, Korea, Greece, Formosa, the Philippines, Venezuela, Dominica, and all the rest of the sixty-odd serf states which are euphemistically referred to as U.S. "client" states. Note with particular attention that most of these U.S. "client" states are run by military, aristocratic, or political juntas of a totalitarian nature — juntas whose prime allegiance is to the hungry Eagle, rather than to their own peoples: juntas, many of which are maintained in power *by* the United States through classic applications of the principles of bribery, blackmail, subversion . . . and armed force.

Or, if you find such a mass of evidence too complex for easy assimilation, take a long look at Vietnam instead. Observe, if you dare, the fantastic and fearful similarities between the way the United States is behaving in that small and benighted country and the way Hitler behaved in *his* heyday.

Having done one or the other — preferably both — I ask you to consider the reality behind the American claims (ably supported by such pillars of righteousness as our own Paul Martin) to being the world's greatest defenders of democracy. Democracy? My God, it is to laugh . . . but bitter laughter it must be since demonstrably the United States is currently engaged in almost every form of domestic and external brutality, aggrandizement, degradation of the individual, and destruction of freedom which, so the U.S.A. maintains with a straight face, are the *singular* hallmarks of the beast called communism.

And what, you say, is this tirade in aid of? Well, it is intended to ensure that you harbour no further illusions about living in a democracy or of being protected by one. You, my son, are a helot, born and bred under the aegis of the United States, and you had damned well better come to terms with this inescapable fact. The illusion of democracy is one that you and your generation can ill afford to nurture. You must recognize that hard reality which not all the cherry-flavoured words of all the hucksters in the world can adequately conceal — you are a serf, no more than that . . . and Massa lives away down south.

You must rid yourself of this delusion because, as I see things, there is no guarantee that the privileged position presently enjoyed by Canadians as "most-favoured serfs" will last. The day is near when the Yankees will see no further need to pamper us — they'll own us outright. And then we may expect to be subjected to the same forms of direct oppression that have been inflicted on most of the other peoples inhabiting the two American continents. The steady growth of overt totalitarianism within the Master State itself brings ominous intimations that the good, fat days for the people who sold themselves into bondage may even now be drawing to a close. And remember — a man who sells *himself* into slavery does not earn the gratitude of his master: instead he earns a deep contempt. We Canadians have well earned such contempt — and a wise slave knows that a contemptuous master is more to be feared, in the long run, than an angry one.

Which leads me to an aside I think worth making. Not *all* Canadians have sold themselves. As you are well aware, the French-Canadians in Quebec don't share our desire for self-immolation. They are resisting and thereby rousing our particular hatred and resentment. Why so? It is not because we really fear the development of a true federation of two nations (many other countries live with such federations, and live well); it is because we are deathly afraid that the intransigence of Quebec will draw the cold and hooded stare of the Eagle and thereby expose *us*, by implication, to the furies meted out to helots who revolt.

What I am trying to tell you is that nobody can, at this late stage, reverse the tide. Quebec, bravely as she may struggle, will fail. And so your own survival now depends on your becoming as selfishly inclined, as amoral as the men who have brought you and this country to its present sorry pass. You must needs become one of them, and you might as well become one of the overseer class, if you can make the grade. I recommend that you enter politics. Although you have not yet displayed the requisite capabilities for duplicity, cowardice, self-serving, and betrayal which pass for morality in high places, you might improve with practice. It is at least certain that a political career is one of the few available that will permit you to enjoy, with any security of tenure, the benefits accrued by renegades and sycophants.

You might conceivably consider entering the business

world, as an alternative, but the opportunities it offers are strictly limited. This is the Holy of Holies, and since its true hierarchy is almost exclusively composed of citizens of the Master State (whether they are card-carrying citizens or only *de facto* citizens is of no import), the chances of a helot rising to those secure seats of power are almost nonexistent. But as a politician you would be employed in the services of the Business God, and as a valuable and trusted slave, you would be deserving of good treatment and assured of a safe niche.

There is another course you might consider taking. You could follow the example of so many of your compatriots and anticipate events by journeying to Rome, before the Marines come north for you. As a beginning you could voluntarily enlist in the legions of the Eagle and thereby gain the jump on those of your generation who do not yet realize that the day approaches when the Ottawa satraps will join Australia, New Zealand, and other such in sending levies to fight America's wars for her. Since you have no Negro, Indian, Eskimo, or other dubious blood in your veins, you ought to be able to wangle a cushy job far from the sound of battle and from the stench of burning babies. Eventually you could hope to be rewarded with citizenship in the Master State, and although this would require that you reject all you have heretofore been taught to believe is good in man, it would at least provide you with something you never had before — a verifiable nationality.

I have only suggested a few of the possible funk holes, and you will easily think of many more. The point is that you *should* be thinking about them very seriously, and right now. Time is running out for your fellow slaves who, complacent and myopic as they are, believe they have made a splendid bargain with a kindly master. The cold and brutal hour when they learn the truth, and when they learn the price of their betrayal of themselves and of their land, lies close at hand. God help them then, for no one else will wish to, if they could.

The Testament of a Canadian

Peter C. Newman

At one of those private diplomatic dinners held in Ottawa during the fall of 1964 — just the sort of occasion when Mike Pearson is at his civilized best — the Canadian Prime Minister entertained his companions, who included Dean Rusk, the U.S. Secretary of State, with a brief but telling anecdote. It involved *The Times* of London's treatment of a particularly gruesome sex crime that took place while Pearson was serving with the Canadian High Commission in the U.K. *The Times* concluded its report with the prim observation that the dead girl had been found in Hyde Park "decapitated and dismembered, but not interfered with."

At the end of the story, Pearson leaned forward to make his point: "That's the way we Canadians feel about you Americans. You can decapitate us and you can dismember us, just so long as you don't interfere with us."

I've always thought that this story summed up exactly my own feelings about the Americans and their influence here. I don't really mind if the Americans own Canada — they own most of the lucrative factors of production in the world anyway — but I object like hell to any attempt of theirs to run us. (Such as the recent statement by U.S. Secretary of the Treasury Henry Fowler, for example, that international corporations not only have commercial importance but a highly significant role in U.S. foreign policy.)

"Canada is not," as Professor W. L. Morton has noted, "a second-rate United States, still less a United States that failed. Canadian history is rather an important chapter in a distinct and even unique human endeavour: the civilization of a northern and arctic land. Because of its separate origin on the northern frontier, Canadian life to this day is marked by a northern quality and a strong seasonal rhythm. The line which marks off the frontier from the farmstead, the wilderness from the baseland, the hinterland from the metropolis, runs through every Canadian psyche."

This, it seems to me, is the right approach to the search for a Canadian identity: that we can find ourselves in the land.

What it consists of — this Canadianism of ours — is a kind of pride that we are here, that we have survived. We may be a nation in trouble, but we are here, and it is our vast, mute geography that has made us unique. It has given us all a feeling that there is a kind of valour in us, in our stand against the grey and black and white of the winter, against the vastness of the land.

The struggle that has formed our national character has not been a contest against other people but against the elements, against the cold and the wind and the stubborn rock. This is a clean battle, but it yields no victories, only the postponement of defeats.

I suppose that any man asked about his homeland can utter wild and chauvinistic declarations — "my country right or wrong" — but I can only speak for myself. Twice in my life I have chosen to be a Canadian — and by implication not to become an American.

In 1940, running away from the Nazi horrors, I came here and not to the United States; since then, like most outspoken journalists of my generation, I have been offered lucrative editorial positions south of the border, and on each occasion I opted to remain — proudly — a Canadian.

While I am tremendously fond of Americans as individuals, I find myself increasingly alienated from their society. I can see in this country, but not in theirs, the possibility of the realization of an ideal. We are a gentler people, a new and uncrowded society — something that must have been true of the U.S. in the 1880's.

Our power structure is not rigid; it is open to anyone with ability and ambition. We are a country that is in the process of becoming; the aura of the frontier is still with us.

Every country is a mystery composed of the lives of many men. And it is doubtful if any other nation is poised more delicately on the edge of perpetual collapse. But I have lived as a Canadian, and I will die as a Canadian — and this, perhaps, is the extent of the testimony that any of us can give to our native land.

Backdrop
Addresses Cowboy

Margaret Atwood

Star-spangled cowboy
sauntering out of the almost-
silly West, on your face
a porcelain grin,
tugging a papier-mâché cactus
on wheels behind you with a string,

you are innocent as a bathtub
full of bullets.

Your righteous eyes, your laconic
trigger-fingers
people the streets with villains:
as you move, the air in front of you
blossoms with targets

and you leave behind you a heroic
trail of desolation:
beer bottles
slaughtered by the side
of the road, bird
skulls bleaching in the sunset.

I ought to be watching
from behind a cliff or a cardboard storefront
when the shooting starts, hands clasped
in admiration,

but I am elsewhere.

Then what about me

what about the I
confronting you on that border
you are always trying to cross?

I am the horizon
you ride towards, the thing you can never lasso

I am also what surrounds you:
my brain
scattered with your
tin cans, bones, empty shells,
the litter of your invasions.

I am the space you desecrate
as you pass through.

The North American Pattern

Mordecai Richler

As I have little that's fresh to say about the United States and our relationship to it, I'm obliged to reiterate here arguments previously published.

A truism or two first.

Canada has not one, but two cultures. If the French is cocooned by language, the English, we are told again and again, is threatened by American-made vileness. For years Faulkner, *Classic Comics*, Ed Sullivan, *Partisan Review*, Elvis Presley, Henry Miller, and Huckleberry Hound have all been spilling freely over the border, stupefying our young ones; but recently Canada has grown resentful. Canadians, without yet building an Uhuru Stadium, unless Expo qualifies, have become proud to be . . . well, Canadians, and the upshot has been an increasingly truculent, occasionally touching national pursuit of something or other we can be true to. A heritage. A tradition. *Anything*.

What is so embarrassing is that while we are determined to defend our culture against any comer, nobody is sure what our culture is, how it differs from the British or American, or come to think of it, if we even have one. Once we were content with a modest but coy definition. We were neither British nor American, but something else. Something nice, very nice. The continued quest for that "something very nice" has created one of the few original Canadian enterprises, the What-Is-Our-Identity business, and a spiteful subsidiary, anti-Americanism.

Alas, I'm not anti-American. Far from it. As a boy in Montreal I can remember that my family was convinced that

12

we gained from dissension between Canada's two cultures, and we looked neither to England nor to France for guidance. We turned to the United States. The real America.

What America, America meant to us in those days was Roosevelt, the Yeshiva College, Danny Kaye, a Jew in the Supreme Court, the *Jewish Daily Forward*, Max Baer, Mickey Katz records, Dubinsky, Mrs. Nussbaum of Allen's Alley, and Gregory Peck looking so cute in *Gentleman's Agreement*. Why, in the United States a Jew even wrote speeches for the president. Returning cousins swore they had heard a cop speaking Yiddish in Brooklyn. There were the Catskill hotels, Jewish soap operas on the radio, and above all, the earthly pleasure grounds, Florida. Miami! No manufacturer had quite made it in Montreal until he was able to spend a month each winter in Miami.

We were governed by Ottawa, we were also British subjects, but our true capital was certainly New York. Success was (and still is) acceptance by the United States. For a fighter this meant a main bout at Madison Square Garden, for a writer or artist, praise from New York critics, and for a businessman, a Miami tan. During the war, in Montreal, our heroes were largely American or American-made. We understood intuitively, for instance, that no Canadian soldier ever would have snarled, "Send us more Japs!" He might have come up with, "No offense to peoples of Asian extraction, but I think we could cope with more Japanese here." Our hearts went out, not to the Black Watch, but to John Wayne and the U.S. Marines. Others precious to us were John Garfield, Joe Dimaggio, and Frank Sinatra, and the most serious crisis of the war was the ban on American comic books, which meant that we were deprived of *Captain Marvel* and *The Batman* for the duration and had to put up with drab Canadian imitations.

It was nice, very nice, that Walter Pigeon, *Canadian-born*, was a Hollywood star, but if you wanted Lauren Bacall you had to be Bogart. An urban American.

By the time we reached university we were, as I recall it, thoroughly embarrassed to be Canadians. Charged with it, we always had a self-deprecating joke ready. Then one or perhaps two of us dared to say out loud, "I'm going to be a writer." The immediate rejoinder was, "What, you're going to be a Canadian writer?" It was a confession of limitations, not an honourable ambition.

As recently as 1960, when I returned to Canada after several years abroad, I found that many Canadians were still prepared to blame the Americans for all our failures. If only *they* would leave us alone, we would be big, important, and above all, cultural. We were urged to buy (and read) Canadian magazines, which were being driven into the ground by "unfair" American competition. "If the Canadian magazines are allowed to die," a concerned Hugh MacLennan said, "we would become the northern equivalent of a banana republic." But among those publications seeking shelter under a cultural umbrella, *Chatelaine*, a specialist in recipes and royalty stories, was typical. The sad truth was, and still is, that most educated Canadians would rather pay more for American periodicals than have the best Canadian magazines, because without them we would feel intellectually cut off.

As Morley Callaghan once said, "The effort to direct our culture away from the sources of light is all very well for speeches by ministers of education . . . but it has nothing to do with the real problem . . . . Canada is a part of the North American cultural pattern . . . . We have our own idiosyncrasies up here, you know, our own peculiar variation of the culture pattern . . . . But it is still definitely American."

Living in London for so long, as I have, the lesson, if it ever had to be learned, is that we Canadians are North American by tradition and culture, and, compared to how foreign we are in England, the difference between, say, a Torontonian and somebody from Denver is no more than a regional nuance.

When I return to Canada from time to time, what I always find most tiresome is the cultural protectionism, the anti-Americanism. No heritage is worth preserving unless it can survive the sun, the mixed marriage, or the foreign periodical. Culture cannot be legislated or budgeted or protected with tariffs. Like potatoes. I also feel it's time we recognized that the best, as well as the worst, influences in the world reach us from the United States, and furthermore, it is most likely that we will always be an American satellite.

However, if I still feel the longest unmanned frontier is an artificial one, I no longer look forward, as I once did, to the day when it might disappear and we would join fully in the American adventure. Vietnam and Ronald Reagan, among other things, have tempered my enthusiasm. Looked at another way, yes, we *are* nicer. And suddenly that's important.

Dat ol' man river

Eric Nicol

Flow of U.S. Capital Vital to Canada
                    —Canadian economist

Roll on, O mighty river
of U.S. dollars, majestic currency
coursing northward into Canada,
holy Ganges of gold
which, even as we defile thee,
(emptying our bladder of self-assertive
sound and fury,
voiding Canadi-anal matter),
yet do we drink of thee
like thirsty geese a-gargling,
and carry thee to the banks
our modest urnings,
and reverently strew upon thee ashes
of identity.

Hail! fructifying effluence,
whose every flood is our good fortune,
depositing the silt of safe investment
wherein we grow our crop of shares,
irrigating the plain
of the world's second highest
standard of living, wherefrom we glean
our simple harvest
of hi-fi and freezer, Jag and yacht.
(Consider the telies, how they grow.)

Let us call thee Jordan
most capital of flows, whose apostles
have witnessed thy wonders
in the *Wall Street Journal*,
and upon whose bounteous bosom
is born each wave of prosperity.
Be not damned by the eager beaver
building his watery cache
of what's Canadian,
but inundate us yet and
yet again, and farther still,
pouring in the pelf until at last
this land is totally submerged.
"Bless thee!" cries our nation.
"Drowning *is* a pleasant sensation."

Cape Breton Is The Thought Control Center of Canada

Ray Smith

Why don't we go away?
Why?
Why not?
Because.
If we went away things would be different.
No. Things would be the same. Change starts inside.
No. Change can start outside.
Possibly.
Then, can we go away?
No. Perhaps. All right. It doesn't matter.

* * *

So you believe in Canada and you're worried about American economic domination? But you can't understand international finance? What you do know is that a landlord can give a tenant thirty days to get out, eh? And the tenant can stay longer if he has a lease, but you don't recall having signed a lease with the Americans?

So you're saying to yourself: "What can I do? What can I do? I can't influence Bay Street . . . . What can I do? . . ." Well . . . thought of blowing up the Peace Bridge?

* * *

The Americans are loath to fight without a divine cause.

Assume we provide this by electing an NDP government, stirring ourselves up with anti-American slogans like: "Give me Liberty or give me Death!" or (the most divine of all) passing legislation which is prejudicial to American money.

With their divine causes, the Americans would destroy our Armed Forces in one week. (This makes a fine game; you can play it out on a map.) Canada will have ceased to exist as a free nation. Now: *think of the fun you'd have in the Resistance!* It's a great subject for daydreaming: be the first kid on your block to gun down a Yankee imperialist.

* * *

You mean you like getting bum-fucked by bald eagles?

* * *

Consider the Poles. They have built a nation which, if not great and powerful, is at least distinct.

Of course, the Poles have their own language, and they have been around for a thousand years. But they have survived despite the attentions paid them by their neighbours, the Russians and the Germans.

Analogies are never perfect, but the Poles do have what we want. Consider the Poles; consider the price they have paid and paid and paid.

* * *

Resistance: Rocky Mountains
You can't see up through the mist (up through the high timber where the air is clean and good), but you know the sun is already gleaming cold on the snowpeaks; soon it will reach down here and burn away the mist, and then it will be too late. Where the hell is that bloody supply column? You hunch forward between the rock and the tree and peer into the gloom. The armoured car escort will appear . . . there: when it gets . . . there Mackie and Joe will heave the cocktails and when the flame breaks Campbell will open up with the Bren . . . . Christ, you hope you get some arms out of this

19

because if you don't you'll have to pack it up soon . . . . Christ, it's cold, your joints can't take much more of . . . a growl from down around the bend . . . a diesel growl . . . .

* * *

Do you love me?

Yes, I love you. You're my wife.

Why did you say, You're my wife?

Uhh . . . .

You said it because you think just because I'm your wife you have to love me when really it has nothing to do with it.

Perhaps. It's more complicated than that.

It's always more complicated. Why can't it be simple? You always say things are too complicated when what you really mean is that you don't want to talk to me. Why can't things be simple?

They are. I love you. As simple as that. So simple there's no point talking about it.

Complicated too, I suppose.

So complicated that to talk about it would always over-simplify it. It's the same with everything.

Then what . . . . Oh! You're impossible to talk to.

You know that isn't true.

Yes.

So . . . .

Then what is important?

Doing.

Doing what?

Heh-heh-heh . . . .

Mmmmm . . . .

* * *

Resistance: Alberta

". . . like a horse's arse!" Einar finishes. You all laugh be-cause Einar tells a good joke and because you're all damned scared as the car flees through the prairie night. "And what about the girl from . . . ." Suddenly the night is day . . . silence . . . then the roar . . . someone gasps, "Jeesus, did we really do that?" You stop the car and stare back down the road at the towering flames . . . another flash . . . its roar . . . and again . . . thousands of gallons of oil . . . . "Well," says Einar, "now I seen the Jeesley sun risin' in the west. I guess I can die happy." Your laughter shakes some sense back into you: you'd better get the hell out of here or you'll maybe die Jeesley quick . . . .

* * *

Resistance: Manitoba
A distant whirr and three more flights of geese knife south through the big Manitoba sky. There was a day when you might have shot at the geese. Now you're waiting for something else to come down the wind through the sedge; there it is, not geese, but eagles, the peculiar aroma of Lucky Strike tobacco and a Texas accent quietly cursing the mud . . . .

* * *

Well, I suppose we could move to England.
I hate England, you know I hate England. It rained and rained . . . .
Oh hell, it didn't rain that much; that was just overcast and occasional drizzle. Besides, we were there in March and April.
Well, it was so dirty. God. I don't mean filth, you know, just . . . grime . . . centuries of grime on everything . . . .
But the pubs, don't forget the pubs.
Sure, I know, but who wants to spend every evening drinking beer?
Yeah, I suppose.
Perhaps we could move to the States.
Be serious.
I was only joking.

* * *

Resistance: Ontario Industrial
"Then *boom!*" cries Johnny. "Boom and the plant got no roof anymore, eh? Ha-ha-ha!" The smoky room fills with laugh-

ter. Johnny knows no fear . . . but no nothing else either. When will they ever learn? You'll try again; your fist hits the table. "A big boom? Fine. Great. So the papers photograph it for the front page, and it's producing again the next day. But two pounds of plastic at the right place on a few essential machines, and this joint won't put out a pound of steel for two years . . . ."

*   *   *

Well then, consider the Poles. Or, consider one Pole. Consider Count Z. Count Z. is a Pole: *ergo*, a Polish patriot. He has his fingers into both the defense and foreign affairs pies. Perhaps he is prime minister, perhaps an *éminence grise*. At forty he is vigorous, experienced, and intelligent.

From the window of his office, Count Z. gazes down into the bustling streets of Warsaw. Fifteen years of peace have prompted a cultural revival. In the near distance, several lines of new smokestacks puff their evidence of Poland's stable and bullish economy. Count Z. shades his eyes; in the far distance the wind washes over the wheat fields which, in two months' time, should become the third bumper crop in three years.

Yet Count Z. is not happy. Of course he is proud to be leading Poland to a new prosperity. But the peasants on his estate have been whispering an old saying: the Pole only buys new clothes so he'll look respectable when he commits suicide. Count Z. sighs and sits down to his work: how can I commit suicide today? (Count Z. has a subtle and self-deprecating sense of humour.)

An aide enters with the foreign office reports. Count Z.'s ambassadors in the Balkans say the Germans and the Russians are supplying arms and money to opposing factions in Bulgaria, Hungary, and Rumania (or whatever they were called in Count Z.'s time). The tension is moderate but unstable. Count Z. frowns.

Next day the Count looks through an economic estimate sheet. Trade with Germany will increase by $12^{1}/_{2}$ per cent over the next year. This is because of a Polish-German trade agreement of two years ago. Count Z. smiles.

But next is the latest note from St. Petersburg. A deadlock has been reached in talks over the disputed ten square miles of Pripet marshland. Resumption of talks is put off indefinitely. Count Z. frowns.

Another aide enters and hands Count Z. a report on Polish defenses. He scrutinizes it although he already knows what it will say: both the eastern and western defense lines are out-of-date and out of repair. To construct new ones would require half the capital in the country. Financially, given five years, one could be constructed. Diplomatically, however, both must be built at once so as not to risk provoking (or tempting) either the Germans or the Russians. Count Z. sighs. If he were English, he would jerry-build something. But in the holy name of St. Stanislaus, how can he insult his Poland with jerry-building?

A visitor is announced: the paunchy, guffawing, monocled Baron Otto von und zu something-dorf who was instrumental, from the German end, in working out the trade agreement. After four of his own utterly unfunny and incomprehensible jokes, the German says:

"But my dear Count Z., Poland a Defense Line in the East against the Depredations of the savage Cossack Hordes wishes to build I understand, ja? Your friendly German Cousins — in the Spirit which the Trade Agreement possible was made — the Cost of this Defense Line to share would be willing. We Germans, as you well know, *Kultur* love, and we to Civilization a Duty consider it Mankind from the Ravenings of the Bear to protect. . . ."

"Sharing only the cost?"

"Well . . . ho-ho-ho . . . of course, we a few Divisions to garrison . . . Transportation Arrangements . . . Security Measures would want . . . ho-ho-ho, and to a slice of Liverwurst yourself help . . . ."

A few minutes after Baron Otto has gone, Prince Igor is announced. Prince Igor is lean and foppish. Only the most delicate efforts prevented his being recalled last year when a prostitute was found beaten to death. He speaks elaborately epigrammatic French, using the occasional Russian phrase to illustrate the quaint wisdom of the peasants.

"*Mon cher* Count Z., I have heard from Petersburg of the

unfortunate breakdown in talks. Of course, love shall always exist between the Tzar and his beloved Slavic cousins. . . . The fat Prussian loves war . . . . As a token of his esteem, the magnanimous Tzar wishes his gallant Polish brothers to take immediate and indisputable possession into perpetuity of the invaluable ten square miles of Mother Russia. In addition, our mutual father wishes to build for his valiant Polish children a defense line along the Polish-German (ah, that term, it disgusts me: *c'est une mésalliance,* the union of an eagle and a pig) border . . . . But will you have a sip of vodka?"

Prince Igor returns to his villa where he finds his aides taking practice shots at the neighbours' cattle. He tells them of his subtle joke: both the pig and the eagle are interchangeable symbols of Germany and Poland.

This subtlety has not been lost on Count Z. He takes a last look at the bustling streets, the puffing smokestacks, and the waving wheat which may or may not get harvested . . . .

In the following weeks Count Z. more and more frequently plays host to Baron Otto and Prince Igor. As politely as possible he explains that he prefers Polish sausage to liverwurst, that vodka upsets his digestion. Baron Otto tells jokes as funny as millstones; Prince Igor weaves his chinoiseries. They smile till their jaws crack; they drop theatening innuendoes.

Count Z. broods. His wife and his mistress both comment on the pallor of his complexion. He will not be consoled. When he looks into the streets below his office, his eyes imagine a scene filled with arrogant, swaggering Prussians or cruel, drunken Cossacks. Tension is mounting in the Balkans: a Russian dragoon and a German uhlan have fought a duel in Sofia. The salons are hissing with rumour.

Baron Otto and Prince Igor deliver their ultimatums on the same day. Accept the liverwurst, not the vodka; accept the vodka and not the liverwurst, or else. Count Z. takes a last glance out the window and sighs. At least they got the harvest in. He rejects the offers. Three weeks later he is cut down while leading a hopeless cavalry charge.

Some time later Baron Otto and Prince Igor sit down together in what used to be Count Z.'s office. They agree that the treacherous Poles are a blot on humanity; else why did they start a war they were sure to lose (as has been proven)? Baron Otto and Prince Igor agree to divide Poland, using the lines where their armies met as a basis for discussions. There will be no arguments over a few square miles here and there, for Poland is a ravaged wasteland. Of course the harvest will be seized to feed the occupying troops: the Poles are pigs, let them root in the ground for acorns if they are hungry. Prince Igor accepts some liverwurst; Baron Otto praises the vodka.

The Balkan situation is smoothed out. The Germans begin building a defense line along the eastern border of their Polish provinces; the Russians begin building a defense line along the western border of their Polish provinces. These lines will take ten years to build (the Polish slaves are so lazy). When they're finished both the Germans and the Russians will want to test the lines. They will go to war. The war will rage back and forth across Poland until . . . .

But let the reader construct the rest. Polish history is very simple in this way. The Poles also are simple: they love Poland.

*　　*　　*

Resistance: Montreal
Curfew for civilians is long past. You sit hunched by the window listening to the laughing soldiers staggering back to their billets. *Espèce de chameaux:* they cannot take a Molson *bleu;* it is too strong for them. If you were allowed in the *tavernes* you would show them . . . . "*Allons,*" whispers Jean-Paul. Silently, silently you slide the window up and wait as the others slip onto the roof. You follow, letting the window slide down behind you. You must hurry; already the others are onto the next roof and creeping toward the fourth house along where the CIA is holding Marc prisoner . . . .

*　　*　　*

Visit/ez EXPO 67

*　　*　　*

Uhh . . . I guess I'd better tell you I don't like eggs fried in butter.

But . . . but . . . .

I'm sorry, but it's true.

But . . . ohh, why the hell didn't you tell me before? God, all this time I've been frying your eggs in butter and . . . .

I didn't want to hurt you.

Well, why did you tell me now? Do you want to hurt me now?

No. Of course, you might have decided all by yourself, but if I have any more eggs fried in butter, the cumulative hurt to me (and of course to you) will have been more than the single sharp hurt of telling you. Do you see?

Ohh . . . .

It took a long time to decide when was the right moment . . . .

Yes . . . yes, I see. Yes. It was the right thing to do.

I love you.

Oh! I love you.

*　　*　　*

Resistance: Maritimes

"Are you sure it's the right cove?" whispers the man in the trench coat. "Keep shut," mutters Willard. Willard is being tough, but it's for the stranger's own good; he wouldn't like going ashore to the wrong reception party. Still, he's got a right to be nervous: it's an hour since you cut the *Rachel B's* engine and no light yet. You peer through the gathering fog. If they don't show in five minutes, you'll have to take the man in the trench coat back to the mainland, and that'll mean coming back again and again until you see . . . the light: one long, three short . . . one long, three short. You answer: two long, two short. "Take her in, Willard," and the man in the trench coat fumbles with his suitcase while Willard dips the muffled oars into the slick black water . . . .

*　　*　　*

North America is a large island to the west of the continent

of Cape Breton.
(Pronounced: Caybrittn.)

*   *   *

Resistance: Women
So what if you have to stay at home with the children? Lots of women in France fought in the Résistance; you can do your part too. Take the church supper tonight, for instance. All those National Guardsmen from New Jersey just got homesick; they wanted a homecooked meal. So Mrs. Parsons said to their commandant, "Why, Colonel, we've always been friendly with your people, living so close to the border. I'm sure the Ladies' Auxiliary would love to give your boys a meal . . . ." The commandant didn't object when you were chosen to make the soup, and he still doesn't know you've planned a very special soup in memory of your Bill, who was shot down in front of his customs shed the day it all began . . . .

*   *   *

Do you love me?
Yes, I love you.
Ohhh!
What now, hmmm? Come here.
Oh.
What? Eh? What is it?
The . . . the way you said it . . . .
Said what?
You know, the way you said I love you.
What about it?
You know very well — you didn't mean it.
I did so . . . really.
No, you didn't. You hardly looked at me, and you went right back to reading your book.
I did mean it. You see . . . hell, I hate explaining . . . .
(He explains for half an hour. The burden of his thesis is that married love is different from single people love. Thus, he loves her twenty-four hours a day, loves her in

such a way that it affects his whole life including the way he pours himself a glass of orange juice in the morning. "It is a love beyond saying," he explains. "I state it in my every action, my every word, my every thought. It is like 'presence' or something." He explains that saying I love you is for single people and that he prefers not to say it except at certain times when he feels for her that simple, heart-throbbing love of single people that comes to him when he watches her hip as she bends over or her hand as she sweeps her hair from her eyes. "At times like that I say I love you." She says she sees and he says, "Do you see?" and she repeats, "Yes, I see.")

I love you.

And I love you .... I love you.

(The question now is whether he will make love to her or go back to reading his book. This question has no answer because the scene is an amalgam of scenes, one each week since they got married a few years ago. But before they do, one little exchange remains.)

Well then, if you didn't feel like saying I love you, why did you say it?

It's better to say it even if it is a technical lie.

What an old funny you are.

Anyway, I love you.

I love you.

*　*　*

See, the way I look at it, your problem is that Joe Yank is the biggest kid on the block. Now I know you're being pretty friendly with him — he being your cousin and all — but someday he's going to say, "Johnny Canuck, my boot is dirty. Lick it."

Now then, are you going to get down on your hands and knees and lick, or are you going to say, "Suck ice, Joe Yank"? Because if you do say "Suck ice," he's going to kick you in the nuts. And either way, you're going to lick those boots. It just depends on how you want to take it.

Of course, you can always kick him first.

* * *

Maybe we could just stay here.
I suppose.
I mean, I like Canada, really. It's not a bad place.
It *is* home.
Perhaps, though, we could go to Montreal for a change.
Could we?
Why not? Drop your Parisian accent and unify Canada.
Ohhh!
We'll have to wait till Expo's over, or we'll never get an apartment; we already have friends there . . . . I don't see why not . . . .
I love you!
Me too!

* * *

The internal walls of an octagonal room are covered with mirrors. In the room stands a man naked. He is an ordinary looking man; other people would say so if they could get in to see him. They cannot get in to see him because they do not know where the entrance to the room is nor, if they did, how to open it. Likewise, the man does not know where the exit is nor how to open it. Possibly he would not use it if he could. Likewise back again, possibly those outside would not enter if they could.

In any case, the man is ordinary looking; but at times he thinks himself surpassingly beautiful and at times surpassingly ugly. The man acts out these conflicting feelings, all the while watching himself in the mirrors. With one hand he strokes his beautiful body; with the other (it holds a whip) he lashes his ugly body. The times when he does these things are, it would seem, all times, and they run concurrently.

The situation lends itself to various interpretations. We might consider them; but let us not.

* * *

For Centennial Year, send President Johnson a gift: an American tourist's ear in a matchbox. Even better, don't bother with the postage.

Eagle's Feather

James M. Minifie

The United States is the glory, jest, and terror of Mankind.

Americans have a deep social conscience, a fervent commitment to simplified ideals, and a low flash point. They passed the Homestead and Land Grant College Acts in the middle of an agonizing civil war. Four-score years later they dedicated twenty billion dollars to restoring a continent through the Marshall Plan. A decade later they embraced Massive Retaliation.

They believe passionately that public business is the public's business and that civil servants should serve and be civil about it; none are better informed than the few or worse informed than the many; their public servants include the most dedicated and brilliant leaders and the most time-serving and venal ward-heelers. They have a spectacular gift for the slogan and an unlimited capacity to use it as an amulet against thought.

They have an urgent desire to be loved and a stock of terror weapons big enough to destroy mankind.

All nations abound in contradictions and tend to preen themselves on those qualities for which they are least conspicuous — viz., the British Empire, French courtesy, German *Kultur*, Italian martial spirit, the Canadian Century, etc. Few advertise their paradoxes with such bravura as the Americans.

Their devotion to free enterprise is matched only by the variety and effectiveness of their governmental controls. Federal supervision of food and drugs, securities, tariffs, and trade functions admirably — far more effectively than Canadian controls.

The Tennessee Valley Authority is proudly displayed to

Visiting Underdeveloped Firemen as a model of state-owned power production, navigation works, flood control, and area rehabilitation, which it is. But so little is it appreciated by Americans generally that President Eisenhower once referred to it as "creeping socialism." At that point anguished screams from John Sherman Cooper, then Republican candidate for senator from Kentucky, caused the White House to revise and extend the President's remarks. It seemed he hadn't meant it that way at all. General Eisenhower is indeed the most respected and voluble champion of free enterprise, although he has not been off the public tit since he was seventeen.

The United States is the greatest socialized state next to the Soviet Union. The U.S. and the U.S.S.R. are proceeding on opposite courses towards and away from governmental control; but don't expect any American to admit this or to trim foreign policy accordingly. Inability to detect and define the obvious, or reluctance to admit it, is the American's weakness. The few great voices who can define and focus issues, like Senator J. William Fulbright, speak their glowing thoughts to an empty chamber; he is as sure as a dinner-gong, as was Edmund Burke in his day. Senator Fulbright can inveigh against the arrogance of power all he likes, but Americans do not think of the United States as an arrogant or an imperial power — despite Okinawa, the Ryukyus, the Trust Territories, and Greenland. They do not think of the United States as a militaristic power, despite Vietnam and the expenditure of seventy billions annually for "defense."

Americans think of the United States as standing up for the right of small nations to decide their own destinies, despite Cuba, the Dominican Republic, Guatemala, Haiti, Nicaragua, et al.

They believe in open diplomacy and the CIA.

They honour the eighteenth century Minute Men and call the Viet Cong terrorists.

At the very time when Newark and Detroit were in flames, a Gallup Poll showed that only one in a hundred questioned thought Negroes had been treated badly; three out of four thought they were treated just like whites.

This political astigmatism has brought the United States to the brink of its most disastrous crisis since the Civil War. A growing Negro minority is demanding a separate state — partition, not apartheid. The White Establishment is concerned but still obsessed with Vietnam, with Castroism, with Che Guevara, with Reds under beds. The Red-necks are armed and trigger-happy, coming close to the old Indian war motto: the only good nigger is a dead nigger.

Americans are capable of the titanic and prolonged effort to assuage the Negroes' discontents, but only if they can discern clearly the facts and the dangers, only if their leadership can inspire them — as John F. Kennedy once did — only if they are willing to forego the self-imposed role of world policemen trying to enforce horse-and-buggy rules in a jet age.

The war in Vietnam is likely to prove as disastrous to the republic as the Sicilian expedition was to Athens, the Negro revolt as dangerous and perhaps more difficult to suppress than the Spartacist revolt to Rome.

Unless Americans can return to the early virtues, principles, and understanding which made them great, Canadians may find to their surprise that their own more elastic union has survived that of the dis-United States.

Open Letter to the Mother of Joe Bass

Margaret Laurence

I don't know what you look like. We will not meet. I don't know how old you are. About my age, I would guess, which is forty-one. I don't know how many kids you have. I have two. My daughter is fifteen, and my son is twelve. You have a twelve-year-old son also.

My son was born in Ghana, and there was no doctor present. The doctor was overworked, and I was okay and normal, so there was only a midwife in attendance. She was a Ghanaian, a matriarch, four kids of her own, and no male doctor could have known what she knew. "It will be a boy," she promised to me as the hours passed by. "Only a man could be so stubborn." When I was in pain, she put out her hands to me and let me clench them, and I held to those hands as though they were my hope of life. "It will soon be over," she said. "Would I lie to you? Look, I know. I have borne." She did know. I had no anaesthetic, and when she delivered him, she laid him, damp and thin and blood-smeared, across my belly. "There," she said. "What did I tell you? Your boy, he is here." She was the only other person present when I looked over God's shoulder at the birth of my son. She had had her children too, and she knew what it was that was happening. She knew that it had to be felt in the flesh to be really known.

In twelve years, so far, touch wood, my son has been lucky. Once in Africa he had malaria, and a few other times, in Canada and England, he had such things as throat infections or chicken pox. Each time I have been afraid in that one-way, guts of ice feeling that I could probably face anything at all except that something really bad should happen to one of my kids.

Now he rides on his bike for countless miles around the countryside. He is a science man at heart, and his electric train set has complicated switches and intricate wiring which he has rigged up himself and which miraculously work and make the miniature engines do as he bids. He has lived life so far among people who were basically friendly towards him. This is not to say that he has never felt pain. He has. More, even, than I know, and I know some of it. But at least until this point in his life, his pain has been something which he could, in some way, deal with by himself.

I have seen your son only once, Mrs. Bass. That was in a newspaper photograph. In Detroit, he went out one evening when his playmates asked him to. It was not an evening to be out. Your son was shot by the police. By accident, the paper said. Shot by accident in the neck. The police were aiming at Billy Furr, who was walking out of Mack Liquors, not with a fortune in his hands but with precisely six tins of stolen beer. When Billy Furr saw the police, something told him to run and keep on running, so he did that, and he was shot dead. But the police had fired more than once, and Joe Bass happened to be in the way. The papers did not say whether he was expected to recover or not, nor how much a twelve-year-old could recover from something like that. A Negro twelve-year-old.

Your son looked a skinny kid, a little taller than my twelve-year-old but not as robust. He was lying on the sidewalk, and his eyes were open. He was seeing everything, I guess, including himself. He was bleeding, and one of his hands lay languidly outstretched in a spillage of blood. His face didn't have any expression at all. I looked at the picture for quite a long time. Then I put it away, but it would not be put away. The blank kid-face there kept fluctuating in my mind. Sometimes it was the face of your son, sometimes of mine.

Then I recalled another newspaper photograph. It was of a North Vietnamese woman. Some marvelous new kind of napalm had just come into use. I do not understand the technicalities. This substance when it alights flaming onto skin cannot be removed. It adheres. The woman was holding a child who looked about eighteen months old, and she was trying to pluck something away from the burn-blackening area on the child's face. I wondered how she felt when her child newly took on life and emerged, and if she had almost imagined she was looking over God's shoulder then.

Mrs. Bass, these are the two pictures. I know they are not fair. I know the many-sidedness of that country in which you live. I know the people I love there, who are more heart-broken than I at the descent into lunacy. Also, I am a North American — I cannot exclude myself from the dilemma. I cannot say *them*. It is forced upon me to say *us*. Perhaps you know who the enemy is — and perhaps it is I.

Once, a long time ago, from the eyes of twenty-two, I wrote a poem about my father, or maybe about the local cemetery, in which the words said, *Under the stone lies my father, ten years dead, who would never know as his, this bastard world he sired.* It did not occur to me then that I would one day stand in that same relation to the world — no longer as a child, but as a parent.

I am not even sure who is responsible. Responsibility seems to have become too diffuse, and a whole continent (if not, indeed, a whole world) appears to be spinning in automation. The wheels turn, but no one admits to turning them. People with actual names and places of belonging are killed, and there is increasingly little difference between these acts and the fake deaths of the cowboys who never were. The fantasy is taking over, like the strangler vines of the jungle taking over the trees. It is all happening on TV.

Except that it isn't. You know, because you felt the pain in your own flesh, that evening when the police shot your son. Is it necessary to feel pain in our own flesh before we really know? More and more, I think that it probably is.

I have spent fifteen years of my life writing novels and other things. I have had, if any faith at all, a faith in the word. *In the beginning was the Word, and the Word was with God, and the Word was God.* The kind of belief that many writers have — the belief that if we are to make our-selves known to one another, if we are really to know the reality of another, we must communicate with what is al-most the only means we have — human speech. There are other means of communication, I know, but they are limited because they are so personal and individual — we can make love; we can hold and comfort our children. Otherwise, we are stuck with words. We have to try to talk to one another, because this imperfect means is the only general one we have.

And yet — I look at the picture of your twelve-year-old son on the sidewalks of Detroit, pillowed in blood. And I wonder — if it were in physical fact *my* son, of the same age, would I be able to go on writing novels, in the belief that this was a worthwhile thing to be doing in this year (as they say) of Our Lord? Mrs. Bass, I do not think I can answer that question.

I am afraid for all our children.

American Apocalypse: Collage with Headlines

Tom Marshall

*"Because to love is frightening we prefer
the freedom of our crimes."*

To the south the violent Utopians rage
at this day. SNIPER KILLS NAZI
Hell's Angels plant the flower girls.
Ahab wants to bomb his leviathan.

HIPPY'S GIRL RAPED BY FIVE NEGROES
At this day. (Can there be a new man?
Can there be a fire that does not consume?
Ahab turn the ship home?)

The whale thrashes in the captain's guts.
(A man alone is terrified by love.)
Love's body is a map of burning flesh.
And poetry is newsprint, not pain.

UFO SIGHTED   STRANGLER THOUGHT INSANE
Love bombs his cities of dark flesh again.

From Roosevelt to LBJ

George Grant

It is hard to contemplate the U.S. with calm these days. The society of comfort and mental health has now its air-conditioned war, presented to us nightly on colour TV. (Air-conditioned, that is, for all Americans except the rural and small-town youngsters who have to do the ground fighting.) At least we did not see Auschwitz till it was over, and anyway it was not English-speaking people who were doing it. Nor can we look at the great republic as outsiders. Go to Stratford, Ontario to hail Canadian drama, but ask on the way which of the factories in Galt or Preston or Kitchener are making the anti-personnel pellets. "With Expo Canada came of age," but (please, Mr. Drury) how much does the swinging city of Montreal make out of the defense sharing agreement? (How absurd anyway to have a fair in praise of twentieth century man without a pavilion on the achievements of technological war.) To think of the U.S. is to think of ourselves — almost.

To think of the U.S. is to remember one's own life. My first political memory is Roosevelt's inaugural in 1933 — being called in from playing in the spring floods and told by my father to listen to the great man on the radio. The creed of the schoolteacher's family was optimistic liberalism, and, oh, with what hope and excitement one listened to FDR in the next decade. The patrician voice called out for a world in which the injustices of the European past would be overcome. It was a liberalism which made a deep appeal to Canadians, partly because underneath its universalism lay the call to the English-speaking peoples to rule the world. Decades later with what nausea one now listens to Roosevelt's inheritors — the Kennedys, the Rockefellers, and Johnson. Yet one knows that these are the true inheritors of that siren voice, both in the society they have built at home and in the empire they have built abroad. The liberal journalists always maintain that America is sound at heart, and it is only the know-nothing reactionaries who lead it astray. Each liberal generation wins its victory over the isolationists, the Nixons, the Goldwaters, etc., etc. But it is those liberal victors who have, more than any others, been responsible for the society as it now is. To try to understand that fact is for me to try to understand the full measure of what it has been to be alive in this era — that is, to make a judgment of the age of progress.

The old platitude must be repeated once again: the United States is the society with the least history prior to the age of progress. (Other societies rush fast to kill what they have, but they still have something to kill.) The basic moral teachers of the United States from Locke to Franklin and from Jefferson to Dewey have been morally shallow. To speak about religion, it is too long and complex a part of European history to describe here why Protestantism's moral teachings have so readily served the deeper springs of modernity. Suffice it to say that the Protestantism of the U.S. became increasingly a legitimizer of the age of progress and its liberalism. And look what that liberalism has done to the older religions of the later immigrant groups — Catholicism and Judaism. (The forlorn hope of Canada once was that from earlier European traditions, British and French, we would maintain moral roots which would allow us to deal more deeply with existence.) Indeed, the highest public hope in the United States was the belief in pluralism —that their society would be made of many streams and that as the society matured these streams would deepen beyond the shallowness of the pioneering moment. But the many streams have all been shallow, and instead of deepening they have been taken up into one great flood. The many shallow streams have widened into one great lake, the defining element of which is belief in affluence through technology.

How can this society of affluence and freedom (freedom about any issue which does not question the basic assumptions) be responsible for the monstrous occurrences in Vietnam? It used to be said: American society may be banal and vulgar, but this at least saves it from the terrible perversions and romantic nihilism of a decaying Europe. But this argument will no longer do, because in the last years the society of affluence and freedom has shown itself capable, not of the maniacal genocide of Auschwitz, but of the bland, impersonal wiping out of an Asian people who could not otherwise be brought to do what American leaders deemed necessary. This is the hardest thing for liberals to understand: how this could arise out of the progressive society they had built. Here I would assert the ancient and forgotten doctrine that evil is, not the opposite, but the absence of good. If your moral roots lead you to exalt affluent technology as the highest end, out of the consequent vulgarity will come a use of power, when deemed necessary to comfortable self-preservation, which perpetrates evil from its very banality. For example, years of accepting manipulative social science have led Americans to seek solutions in pacification programs, the attendant cruelties of which are hardly evident to those who plan them. The emptiness of a moral tradition that puts its trust in affluence and technology results in using any means necessary to force others to conform to its banal will.

To think ill of the dominant American tradition must not allow one to forget that which remains straight and clear among Americans themselves. Living next to them, Canadians should know better than most how incomplete are the stereotyped gibes of Europeans. The cranes and the starlings still fly high through their skies; sane and wise families grow up; people strive to be good citizens; some men still think. Above all, many Americans have seen with clarity the nature of that which chokes them and seek for ways to live beyond it.

The Great Liberal Myth

John W. Warnock

All nation-states live by myths. They are necessary for social cohesion. Yet there is no nation-state in the world today more committed to myths than the United States. The American myths of today are those of eighteenth century liberalism, a philosophy of myths that has died everywhere else but to which the Americans desperately cling.

The United States is the New World where traditional conservatism and power politics are dead. It is the great egalitarian society where everyone is created equal; advancement comes by recognition of ability, and those who do not succeed are judged to have been lazy or not ambitious. It is the nation-state that celebrates Locke and Montesquieu, where the acceptance of pluralism sees to it that no group or class can dominate society. Free enterprise and competition assure that the customer will get the best product at the lowest price. It is the nation of peace that rejects war and imperialism. It is the great melting pot, the haven for oppressed masses, the tired, and the weak. It is the society that has proven Marx wrong. It is the individual's paradise. It is the land of the free. It is the Great Society.

In the past, Americans have felt a profound need for these myths. This is still true today, but there is a rising group in the United States which is finally beginning to accept the truth. Two things in particular have contributed to this: the rebellion of the blacks and the vicious war that is being waged against the Vietnamese.

First, the crisis at home signals the end of one of the great American myths, that the United States is an egalitarian society. In the past, those who have described the existence of a governing class in the United States have been ignored or dismissed. For example, recall the American response to Charles A. Beard's classic work, *An Economic Interpretation of the American Constitution*. All he did was show that the Founding Fathers stood to benefit personally from the political system they created, but this was an attack on a favourite American myth. The same sort of reception greeted C. Wright Mill's *The Power Elite*, which challenged the great American myth of pluralism. A new study by G. William Domhoff, *Who Rules America*, demonstrates the existence of a governing class, the "business aristocracy." But there is no doubt that it will be repudiated by the academic establishment and ignored by the rest of society.

However, the American establishment can no longer adequately deal with criticisms of the American system simply by issuing those familiar pious pronouncements. Even in the United States, it is becoming public knowledge that in the richest country the world has ever known there are vast inequalities of wealth, with millions living in the state of starvation, poverty, and deprivation. There is a growing group of Americans, including some whites, who have decided that they have heard all the words and promises that they want to hear. Like all oppressed people, they have come to the desperate point where they feel that there is no hope for justice except through violence. The rebellion will continue for some years, for the United States as a system cannot easily make the necessary changes — they require a social revolution.

Until the war in Vietnam, the United States was able to maintain a generally favourable image abroad. Many people were willing to believe the myths of the great liberal society. American excesses overseas were seen as exceptions, not as the rule. This is now changing. Yet in the United States the majority of the people still want to believe that their country is a great, progressive, liberating force. How could the United States be an empire? After all, wasn't the United States the first to break away from the old colonial system? American expansion across the continent was not imperialism but Manifest Destiny. Expansion overseas was not for reasons of self-interest but for humanitarian ideals, to uplift, to Christianize, and to civilize backward peoples. The Monroe Doctrine was not the declaration of a sphere of influence but only an announcement that the United States would protect the independence of certain nations. How could anyone suggest that the international free market is a system of exploitation? It is the natural economic system. American investment abroad is really a form of foreign aid and helps underdeveloped countries advance economically. A liberal state cannot be imperialistic. The U.S. has no colonial office. U.S. intervention in other countries has been to resist aggression and always has had the support of the local governing authorities. The United States is defending freedom all over the world.

In the non-Western world there is no uncertainty about the imperial role of the United States today, and even among the European friends of the United States, the myth has been shattered. The Vietnam War has done that. The United States has mobilized the most barbarous military machine the world has seen since Nazi Germany. Yet the mass of Americans must believe that their cause is just — there must be a rationalization, for the alternative is to question the whole basis of their society. Outside the United States, it is common to compare the U.S. war in Vietnam with the French war in Indochina and Algeria. The French people finally were repelled by the horror of the war they were forced to wage, particularly the indiscriminate murder of civilians, torture of prisoners, napalm bombing of villages, and the need to deny traditional basic rights and democratic freedoms to subject peoples. The French people took a moral stand and withdrew. Dean Rusk and other American leaders assure us that the French decision signaled a weakness in that society which is not present in the United States. The Americans will persist, they argue, because they know they are right.

History will note the curious role that academics have played in the United States in maintaining the myths of the establishment. In most countries, academics are the intellectual critics of society, those who are primarily concerned with great moral issues. In the United States, the vast majority of academics have seen their primary role as defenders of the existing system. Thus, they have worked hard to maintain the myth of the pluralistic society; how few critical works of economics and political science have been printed in the

United States. During the cold war, it was impossible to find an article dissenting from the U.S. official foreign policy line in a scholarly American journal. As one writer recently described it, "a hundred flowers have no doubt bloomed, but they have almost without exception been tactical flowers on a single strategic stem." Academic Stalinism is dying hard in the United States.

The great liberal society of the United States is now in a period of real crisis, similar to that of Athens at the peak of that liberal-democratic empire. Will the United States go the way of all previous empires? Will the individualistic society break down because of internal contradictions? The rest of the world would view the future of humanity with a great deal more confidence if the United States did not have nuclear weapons.

The anti-American

A. W. Purdy

— Met briefly in Havana
among the million Cubans waiting
Fidel's speech on May Day 1964
under a million merciless suns
He came around and shook hands
with the foreign visitors
a guy who looked like a service station attendant
in his olive drab fatigues and beret
bearded and smoking a black cigar
— the Argentine doctor and freedom fighter
Che Guevara
And I remember thinking the North Vietnamese ladies
looked especially flower-like beside him
I remember his grip particularly
firm but perfunctory
half politician and half revolutionary
for he had many hands to shake that day

Later he disappeared from Cuba
and there were rumours of quarrels
between himself and Castro
and U.S. newspapers asked nervously
"Where is Che Guevara?"
And some thought he might reappear
in the American South to lead the Negroes
and march with a black army to the green sea
over the snow-white hills and fungus cities
But Havana Radio reported Guevara

had joined guerillas in "a South American country"
spreading the doctrine of world revolution
in accordance with recognized medical practice
And the U.S. expressed some small doubt
about the reliability of Havana Radio
while I thought of him — shaking hands

Back home in Canada I remembered Guevara
along with structural details of Cuban girls
the Grand Hotel at Camaguay with roosters
yammering into my early morning sleep
an all-night walk in Havana streets with a friend
a mad jeep-ride over the Sierra Maestras
where sea-raiders attacked a coastal sugar mill
and Playa Giron which is the "Bay of Pigs"
where the dead men have stopped caring
and alligators hiss in the late afternoon
Again May Day in Havana 1964
with a red blaze of flowers and banners
and Castro talking solemnly to his nation
a million people holding hands and singing
strange to think of this in Canada
And I remember Che Guevara
a man who made dreams something
he could hold in his hands both hands
saying "Hiya" or whatever they say in Spanish
to the flower-like Vietnamese ladies
cigar tilted into his own trademark
of the day when rebels swarmed out
of Oriente Province down from the mountains

"Where is Che Guevara?" is answered:
deep in Bolivian jungles leading his guerillas
from cave to cave with scarlet cockatoos screaming
the Internationale around his shoulders
smoking a black cigar and wearing a beret
(like a student in Paris on a Guggenheim)
his men crawling under hundred foot trees
where giant snakes mate in masses of roots

and men with infected wounds moan for water
while Guevara leads his men into an ambush
and out again just like in the movies
but the good guy loses and the bad guys always win
and the band plays the Star-Spangled Banner

Well it is over
Guevara is dead now and whether the world
is any closer to freedom because
of Che's enormous dream is not to be known
the bearded Argentine doctor who translated
that dream to a handshake among Bolivian peasants
and gave himself away free to those who wanted him
his total self and didn't keep any
I remember the news reports from Bolivia
how he was wounded captured executed and cremated
but first they cut off his fingers
for fingerprint identification later
in case questions should be asked
and I remember his quick hard handshake
in Havana among the tiny Vietnamese ladies
and seem to hold ghostlike in my own hand
five bloody fingers
of Che Guevara

Their America, and Mine

Robert Fulford

Once I spent a golden week in America. It seemed to me that within six magic days I went almost everywhere in the United States I could want to go. I was in Washington, New York, Cleveland, Pittsburgh. I was in Kentucky, Maryland, Delaware, Iowa. I was even in Oshkosh, Wisconsin. And everywhere it was beautiful: the sun was bright and the air bracing, the crops were good, the people were happy and prosperous. It was like a holiday, and I woke every morning full of joyful expectancy.

Just one thing was wrong: the purpose of my visit was Senator Barry Goldwater, whose presidential campaign I was following as a newspaperman. He struck me, in this one-week exposure, as a thoroughly nasty personality. I'd read a dozen times that he was, behind all his unfortunate political ideas, a good man; but as I watched him manipulating the racial fears of the Cleveland people or trying on a little McCarthyism in Wisconsin, I came to the opposite conclusion. By the end of the week, the ideas seemed to me preferable to the man.

At that point, fortunately, Goldwater no longer mattered. The ninety or so reporters who flew in his jets and then trailed after him in press buses had come to regard him with a certain contempt. He was now a sure loser and so (I, for one, tried to believe) was his kind of America — the rotten, half-dead, conservative, paranoid America. Liberal America, *my* America, was winning, easily. I would never have chosen as representative of liberal America the man who was then in the process of beating Goldwater, but I was confident that

Lyndon Johnson was the servant of those American ideals and impulses I trusted most. Goldwater was thus a figure of no real consequence, and I could relax and enjoy my week in his company. Most of the other newspapermen on the plane — liberals, like myself, with one or two exceptions — shared this attitude.

All that was long ago, of course, much longer than the years which chronologically intervened. Everything has changed. It has for a long time been evident that, in some ominous way, Goldwater *won* that election, and we admirers of liberal America lost it.

For anyone who loves the United States, the years since 1964 have been torture. I am, to state a fairly vital point, pro-American. Some good friends of mine are basically suspicious of the American idea, and many Canadians who are otherwise sensible are given to the view that Americans as a class are "immature" or "irresponsible" or just plain obnoxious. Not me. I like America and Americans. I admire them. I've always been profoundly grateful that Canada shares this continent with the American people; God bless America, as I think both Frank Underhill and Marshall McLuhan have said, for saving us from the fate of Australia.

This affection, like most affection, proceeds not from a conscious decision but from my personal history and from the nature of what might be called my interior design. For the fact is that some large part of the furniture of my mind and imagination has always been clearly stamped "Made in U.S.A." My first heroes were American musicians: Ellington, Armstrong, Peewee Russell, later Charlie Parker and Miles Davis. The novelists I first took seriously — Mark Twain, Hemingway, Fitzgerald, Salinger, eventually Bellow — were all American. The painters of my lifetime who have meant most to me have been those same painters who made New York the center of their world: Pollock, de Kooning, Kline. And in my own trade, literary journalism, my heroes (with two major exceptions, Shaw and Orwell) have all been American: Lionel Trilling and Clement Greenberg, Leslie Fiedler and Edmund Wilson, Dwight MacDonald and Murray Kempton. Why, even my favourite English poet, W. H. Auden, has been an American citizen for a long time.

These people, more than any Englishman or Frenchman or Canadian, have taught me what art is, what is going on in the world out there, and who I am. I would not, looking at it objectively, recommend them to anyone else, nor would I suggest them as the basis of a course in civilization. They are merely the basis of *my* sense of civilization, such as it is. Heroes and models, I discovered only a few years ago, *happen* to you; as with parents, you don't choose them. You wake up one morning and discover they are there. You can hardly defend them or explain them, any more than you can defend or explain your parents. Most of mine are American, and that's all there is to it.

Still, I confess to an even deeper pro-Americanism than all this suggests. In the early 1950's, when I was in my 20's, I came to realize — "believe," perhaps, would be a more objective and defensible way to say it, but even so I'll stick with "realize" — that the world was involved in a basic conflict of values and that this conflict involved me. Some people in Moscow, whom I had every reason to despise, were trying to take over the world — *they* said this was so, and I for one believed them. And some people in Washington, whom I had no reason to despise, were opposing them. The issues were complicated, as all issues are, but that was the basic point. Ottawa had little to do with it. London was involved rather more, but was not important. Moscow versus Washington: this was what counted. I knew which side I was on, and through the 1950's, indeed up to (and past) President Kennedy's death in 1963, I had few doubts.

Now, of course, doubts swarm around me. I find myself susceptible to even the most tenuous arguments of the cold war revisionist historians, not because their view of the past is so persuasive but because the present in which I read them is so poisoned. Vietnam is a terrible disaster for everyone involved; the Vietnamese suffer horribly, but what may finally be even worse is that the American spirit, on which so much of the future of mankind depends, is buckling under the strain. American intellectual life, for instance, has gone rotten. The typical American intellectual today is a man who hates the United States and everything for which it stands, who in his heart joins those demonstrators who so enthusiastically pissed on the walls of the Pentagon. Susan Sontag has said America is doomed; her only hope is that it won't pull down the rest of the world when it goes under. The black ideologues are desperate; their white opponents grow more vicious every day. For once, all the people feel that a terrible cloud hangs over them; they differ only in describing its nature — is it communism, is it Johnsonian imperialism, is it Black Power, is it anarchy? Whatever it is, it is breaking the heart of America, and someone in my position can only look on in impotent sorrow. My love for my kind of America is permanent, but can my kind of America endure? For the first time, I now take seriously the possibility that it cannot.

American Girl:
A Canadian View

George Jonas

It is reassuring
To spend part of a night
With an American girl.

Chances are she will not resemble
The leaders of her nation
In speech, figure, or stance:

If she has imperialistic designs
She may draw you without a struggle
Into her sphere of influence.

Then you'll find her battledress
Fit for her private battles,
See not her battleships but hear her battlecries,
And melt (perhaps with a wistful smile)
Before the native napalm of her eyes.

But she'll seem to be prepared
To give as well as to accept
Some foreign aid

And by midnight or so
While the fires of her manifest destiny smoulder
You'll be all ready to slip across
The world's longest undefended border.

Some Feelings About the United States

William Kilbourn

As a child I used to fight out our historic disputes with the Yankees to a more satisfying conclusion. The boundaries of Canada in my battered, red Thomas Nelson Atlas are all redrawn in pencil. Fingers of American land from Maine to the Alaska Panhandle are chopped off and coloured-in Canadian. What I liked best, though, was not the old battles but new ones of my own invention. There is a fury of arrows showing how we captured Minneapolis and Duluth and got back our rightful share — and more — of the Upper Great Lakes' shoreline. I did not know at the time — it was either in 1933 or 1934 and I was seven — that my fantasy was shared in high places; that in fact until its cancellation in 1933, Defense Scheme Number 1, the brainchild of Canada's Director of Military Operations and Intelligence, Colonel J. Sutherland "Buster" Brown, included plans, astonishingly similar to my own, for the capture of American border cities.

At school during World War II, we sophisticates of the Sixth Form pretended to have put away childish things, such as anti-American feelings and old-fashioned Family Compact military enthusiasms. Still, I detected a certain covert pride even among those of us lepers consigned to Platoon IIIC of the College Battalion (the moral equivalent of the Dirty Dozen) in the knowledge that ours was the only Canadian cadet corps which actually possessed battle colours — won for its part in resisting the Irish-American Civil War veterans who invaded Canada in 1866. Today, even more than at school, that absurd and inglorious battle at Ridgeway — so crucial a symbol for the new Dominion's being born — and the account of the solemn funeral gun carriages rumbling through the crowd-lined, black-draped streets of Toronto still rouses in me a twinge of patriotic pride.

And I still resonate over the many little invasions of Canada from the U.S. of a century and more ago when I think of what happened to Guatemala and Cuba and the Dominican Republic during the past decade when they did not remain sufficiently fascist, free-world-loving, neighbourly, or whatever to suit powerful segments of American public opinion. Just suppose that an independent Ontario and Quebec of the future (I can't conceive of the new hardware business culture of the Canadian West doing it), suppose they should be governed by some Canadian brand of Castroism. And suppose, to cope with our new hard-won and unpopular poverty, that our socialist governors should seize the property of American branch firms. Suppose too the abolition of the Ottawa Mind (in case Canada gets to the moon first, Ottawa Man is even now sketching out delicate position papers on how it may be persuaded, after due consultation with Washington, to join NORAD and NATO). I wonder how long it would be before the Marines landed, at the invitation of our old power elite, to make Canada safe once again for the Canadian Manufacturers Association, the Canadian Labour Congress, and the Chamber of Commerce.

Now anger-fantasies of this sort — as irrational in their own way as Buster Brown's — are worth examining. The anger I sometimes feel towards "the Americans" is not that anger mixed with amusement or pity which a Canadian shows towards the British or French when they become caricatures of themselves. Part of my anger undoubtedly stems from sibling jealousy. I admire and covet not only American styles and achievements but also the American's generosity of spirit and willingness to take total responsibility for himself and his actions. A Canadian, by contrast, has been called someone who doesn't play for keeps.

My anger stems partly too from the fact that even the most intelligent Americans, with rare exceptions, neither know nor care that they share this continent with a Canadian culture distinct from their own and that English Canada, now that it has at last cut most of its umbilical ties to the mother country, is for the first time in its 200-year-old history, ready to explore and realize the full dimensions of its peculiarly North American heritage. Since I've just finished an anthology of contemporary writing about the Canadian identity, I won't pursue that theme here. But perhaps one small example is worth mentioning. The difference between the conception, planning, and execution of the New York World's Fair and Expo '67 does suggest several significant differences between the United States and Canada.

Chiefly, however, I can be angry at "the Americans" because I am so American myself. America is my past: most of my ancestors originally came from the United States where they had lived for many generations. America is my foster parent: I lived and worked and studied there for three years; one of my sons is a Yankee. America, from New York to San Francisco, is our change of air and our other place of business. Above all it is our ultimate metropolis, the one that speaks our North American style and serves as a place of refuge when Canadian smugness and pettiness become too hard to take. America is our cultural asylum, just as Canada has been a *political* asylum for American-way-of-life dodgers ever since the underground railway and the United Empire Loyalists.

America provides us with so many of our heroes, from Jefferson and Lincoln to FDR and Kennedy, from Hawthorne to John Cage, Bob Dylan, and Buckminster Fuller. America gives the Canadian writer a usable major past to nourish both his craft and his way of seeing things, a past perhaps even more accessible to us than it is to contemporary American writers. As for speech, Huckleberry Finn invented the American dialect for Canadians as well as for his countrymen. It was certainly not my English-Canadian schoolmasters who encouraged me to say "who to" instead of "to whom." They never gave me permission to try yawping like Whitman or fooling about with *Moby Dick* as the pattern for a book about steelmaking — or to begin another one with the words "Call me Bill." Juvenalia, perhaps, but then a mature Canadian like Jean Lemoyne can find in Henry James and T. S. Eliot not only the imagination to become and to remain a North American, but also the strength to cope with Europe without descending into colonialism. And finally, it was not Governor Simcoe and Doctor Strachan who taught me freedom from the paralysis of the European class system. It was not my five generations of Ontario farm ancestors, though I owe them much, who made me feel that one of the chief blessings of the human condition is to know the privilege of being a North American.

Canada has long been another America, an America in the making, but one with a difference. We still have the chance, in this open, half-formed, dimly identified society of ours, to make something new, even marvelous, out of our American heritage. Not in the way Emerson had in mind a century ago when he turned his back on the whole western tradition ("the storied cliffs of Salamis and Marathon") and proudly proclaimed "We shall be classic to *ourselves*." Nor in Lincoln's sense of being a land that is "the last best hope of earth." There is, after all, a foulness that has flowed in the wake of that divine archaic dream, and it has produced Fortress America and John Birch, Jay Gatsby's friends and Senator Joe McCarthy, not to mention more plausible and therefore more dangerous manifestations like Congressman Mendel Rivers and Richard Nixon's recent statement: "Cuba is the second most powerful nation in our hemisphere." (What in the name of Gotham City did he mean? "Mightier than Mexico, richer than Canada, bigger than Brazil, swifter than Chile — It's a Red! It's a Rocket! It's SUPERFIDEL!")

An un-Canadian activity, thank God, there is no such thing as; it is like the purple cow — something we need never hope to see. Charles Hanly has pointed out that while a good U.S. citizen may plausibly say "I am an American, therefore I am a man," the Canadian patriot can at best state "I am a man, and I am also grateful that I happened to be a Canadian." But that gratitude, one must admit, has not yet shown itself in great achievements. Except for a few outstanding individuals such as Doctors Osler, Banting, and Bethune, or a few groups of people like the Canadians in the contemporary world of the performing arts or the unsung race of Canadian inventors who have helped transform modern technology, we cannot claim that the world would have been a much worse or different place today if there had never been a Canada.

We will in fact only begin to make a contribution matching

our immense potential and unique good fortune when we dare make use of the American heritage that belongs to us. Mel Watkins remarked a couple of years ago that, unlike Britons and Frenchmen and Americans, "Canadian scholars and novelists have not produced major critiques of the American way of life." We are so well-informed about America, so tuned in to the immediate American environment, that we have not perceived its meaning. To let ourselves be "bombarded with the message is almost to preclude understanding of the medium." From his criticism I am sure he excepts two of the great scholars of our time, Harold Innis and Marshall McLuhan, whose theories of communications and civilization have sprung from a study of peculiarly Canadian conditions. But his criticism is otherwise still just as valid as his question: "Are we ready to risk the discovery of America?"

Colonial-minded until the 1960's, Canadians were never in a position to belong to the twentieth century, let alone to pretend that it belonged to us. But we are a society now just beginning to live in the post-modern world of Expo '67. The parallel with the last days of the first Roman Empire is remote but possibly useful. In spite of the corruption at the power center of Imperial Rome, there was a flowering of classical culture in the outlying provinces, Spain and Gaul and North Africa, towards the end of the fourth century. Not only was it good in itself, but it laid the groundwork, before the barbarian tides submerged the Western Empire forever, for the freer civilization of Romanesque and Gothic and Renaissance Europe that sprang from it. We Canadians could still be one of the late redeeming rebel provinces of the *Pax Americana*. We could share, along with its more recent and alien but major heirs in Japan and Europe and with American disaffiliates themselves, the function of seed-bearers for the coming world civilization. The American experience is too precious to be entrusted to present-day American patriots only. The empire of the Romans may be rotting at the core — in the Pentagon and Foggy Bottom, Madison Avenue and the megaversities. But wherever the best of the American heritage has taken root, there is ground for hope. And even on the darkest days, if you will look, you can still see the chimes of freedom flashing.

Vive le Canada Libre

Laurier LaPierre

America is huge. It is this immeasurable vastness that is at once both horrifying and emulatory. Canadians appreciate both the horror and the idle worship, but because Canada is small and, simply, because we are not American, our perspective is partially cleared of the intense, nationalistic, myth-making, flag-waving pressure brought to bear on the American citizen.

Yet America plays an immense role in our lives. The development of our country, the organization of its territory, the rational utilization and development of its natural resources, the regional and individual distribution of the fruits of that development: all of these are becoming more and more impossible. The development of our country is subordinated to the views and to the needs of the United States of America. Hence, Canada is seriously handicapped, and its social, political, and economic problems will never be solved adequately until the absentee landlords stop dominating the country. As a people, we must buy back our autonomy and rediscover that liberty which must be the lot of mankind.

Yet this view to many Canadians is a myth. Due to tremendous pressure — political, economic, social, etc. — our objectivity is tainted. Canada's taint is principally social — theatre, dress, radio and TV, film, books, resultant philosophies, ways-of-life, and so on. Britain's taint is economic competition. And the economic gifts of the United States, along with correlative pressures, severely warp the perspectives of India, Africa, and Southeast Asia in one way or another. For the sake of conciseness, generalization is obviously necessary: America pervades almost every culture in almost every conceivable fashion. One beauty of this phenomenon is that it raises both hackles and national pride in the smaller nations. Let us examine the Canadian reaction as symbolic of others.

Geographical statistics apart, America is huge and Canada small. In a very real way, Canada represents the attitudes of many other less developed countries towards her vast southern neighbour. Canada, like most other countries, recognizes both the possible goods of capitalism and, at the same time, the rottenness, propaganda, and double standards which actually emanate from it, insidious and omnipresent as the sweat that American sprays, creams, and roll-ons were invented to eradicate. Double standards are as natural as perspiration. But our small, well-to-do country manages to reject — idealistically if not practically — most of the smell.

We fight the American way with our own stockroom myth: the Quebec Fact, the French-Canadian Fact, the Canadian Fact. Why do we need to do this? Why are there in fact differences; why does Canada still exist; why do we hope to retain a distinct — though similar — identity? And lastly, why does Canada in many ways symbolize many of the really deep-rooted apprehensions of smaller developing countries?

Culture — indefinable but omnipresent — is the product of everything that a country is. Money, crime, war, power, a sense of individuality (there really is no end to the cultural horizons of America) all add to the Way. Canada looks on with detached amusement and envy. At Expo the truth was revealed. In the gigantic geodesic sphere, the world saw pictures of film stars, baseball hats, Elvis Presley's guitar on special loan, Marines from Vietnam with pictures of Mother and God in their wallets, apple pie crumbs sticking to their white cotton gloves. Ah! That was democracy at its finest! Sound, fury, glamour, and the lollipop all in one round package! This was the American Dream. Canadians saw the Marines without war, the CIA, death, destruction, horror. We saw candy without the cavities, heroes and martyrs without the millions of destitute and dead that gave them the honour.

The intellectuals protest: draftcards burn with the babies; the Left talks like Negroes; Negroes resist assimilation; beatniks, vietniks, peaceniks, whiteys, ethnics grow older, less desperate, and tune in to the Way. You can't fight it. It's too huge. Like the Land-Surveyor in Kafka, you never really find the castle. Because you *are* the castle. And then they send for McLuhan the Expert to teach communications at $100,000 a year!

Canada watches all this on TV, films — every available In-Living-Colour-Media. The Word comes through clearly via every open channel. And Canadians invariably turn up the volume. We dislike their system, abhor their war, protect their refugees. Because (thank Apathy!) we are different. Yet, in 1976, doubtless there will be motorcyclists at Ste. Catherine and St. Laurent wearing Confederate hats, models wearing red, white, and blue! Ah! Let us succumb to the facts! Big Brothers, as Freud and the prime ministers knew well, are to be at once envied and emulated. Let us use as much of the lollipop as possible and return the unused portion for a refund of conscience and pride in Canada. Still, as Gleason would say, how sweet it is! Or de Gaulle: Vive le Québec libre! Or some English-Canadian plagiarist: United we stand . . . .

What then? We have three choices: accept, reject, or be specifically of Canada.

To be of Canada is to acquire pride in this country and in its *real* independence.

To be of Canada is to stop being a parasite and to live with our two feet firmly planted upon the ground, not dreaming of a wealth we do not own, a power we do not have, an international presence we do not make, and a development we do not achieve.

To be of Canada is to be able to say "Vive le Canada libre."

Hymn to the Republic

Irving Layton

They say you have too many hydrogen bombs.
I do not think so: you do not have enough.

They say you have too many ICBM's.
I do not think so: you do not have enough.

They say you have too many soldiers and sailors and airmen.
I do not think so: you do not have enough.

They say you are too rich and too powerful.
I do not think so: you are not rich and powerful enough.

They say your fingers itch with empire and grab.
I do not think so: your sensitive fingers do not itch enough.

Shine on, glorious republic.

I love your baseball heroes, America.
I love your movie stars, America.
I love your pop artists, America.
I love your politicians, America.
I love your great Jewish comics, America.

Land of the brave, home of the free
Defender of human liberty.

Beside you other lands are bad plumbing and rusted toilet
  seats.
Beside you other lands are anaemia and bad breath.
Beside you other lands are privilege and decaying perukes.
Beside you other lands are somnolence and embroidered
  counterpanes.
Beside you other lands are the belch of dictators and ukases.

God bless you, America.

I revere your great presidents, America.
I revere your great generals, America.
I revere your great writers, America.
I revere your great philanthropists, America.
I revere your great rebels, America.

O say can you see!

I'm wild about your hospitality to fearful Russian poets.
& your hospitality to Canadian talent and brains unable to
  find any backers at home.
& your plunging, adventuring financiers and businessmen:
  more power to them at home — and abroad where they're
  especially needed.
& the Negro riots in Buffalo and Detroit.
& President Johnson: in my crystal ball I see seraphim already dusting the golden chair he'll occupy at the right
  hand of Abraham Lincoln.
& Judy Garland and Cassius Clay.
I'm wild about your guts, dash, generosity, your dreams and
  idealism.
I'm wild, America, about your heroic and persistent sense of
  failure.

God bless you, America.

May the Stars and Stripes wave briskly forever;
may it wave from the highest mountain peak,
the breeze bringing to tyrants and terrorists everywhere
a fatal, bone-chilling pneumonia
but to Canadian socialists & nationalists & academic creeps
only the common cold for with us parochialism and stupidity
  are geopolitical

fate for the same reason that moralic acid is the favourite beverage of all
little peoples condemned to crawl between the feet of towering historic giants.
Without its warming taste how could they endure themselves or one another
as croaking in their barren frogponds their round, empty eyes blink across
the surrounding gloom: cowardice is wisdom; mediocrity, sanity; philistinism,
olympian serenity; and the spitefulness of the weak, moral indignation.

> I'm sorry for you, America.
> You deserve grander neighbours
> than assholes covered with ten-gallon hats!

Shine on, glorious republic, shine forever.

Death Chant for
Mr. Johnson's America

Raymond Souster

America
you seem to be dying
America
moving across the forty-ninth parallel each day a stronger
more death-laden stench; wafting inshore from off the
Great Lakes the same unmistakable stink, so unlike the
usual putrefaction of these waters
America
the cracks are beginning to show
America
I knew you were marching to doom the night a young American told me: "There at Buffalo I saw our flag flying, then
fifty yards further on your Maple Leaf, and I thought:
thank God I'll never have to cross that line going back
again."
America
even your best friends of yesterday are now proud to be
your enemies
America
that time is past when the sight of the Stars and Stripes flying
at the masthead of one of your ships can calm the
"natives," that time too is over when a small detachment
of Marines on landing can still quickly restore law and
order and a continuance of the prescribed vested interests
America
there will be no more San Juan Hills, no more Remember
the Maines, no more sad empires of United Fruit

America
your time is running out fast
America
you haven't changed at all since you sent your New York
State farm boys across the Niagara to conquer us once and
for all, since you printed your handbills promising French-
Canadians sweet liberation from their oppressors, since
you looked the other way as Fenians played toy soldier
across our borders
America
you're sitting on your own rumbling volcano
America
only you could create a New York where a new breed of
white rats chase slum children through rotting rooms,
biting infant's flesh with the same relish as that tailor's
dummy at the same moment downtown taking his first
mouthful of ten-dollar steak and beaming across at his
equally overdressed partner as she too presses her careful
teeth into the meat course, only you could create drunks
lying in squads in doorways, addicts readying fixes in dirty
washroom heavens, only you could build these terrifying
buildings reaching up through dirt noise and smog-death
for a breath of clean air somewhere at the thousand foot
level if at all, only you could fashion East River mountains
of used cars, graveyards of King Auto more mysterious
than elephant burial grounds, only you could spawn the
greed the corruption of a Wall Street with its ticker-tape
fortune-cookie dreams and short-sell nightmares, only you
could conceive this monster and only you will be the one
to destroy it pier by pier, block by block, citizen by citizen
America
you seem bent on self-destruction
America
today you are Ginsberg's nightmare brought up-to-date,
today you would sicken Hart Crane, make him puke on
his Brooklyn Bridge, today you are fast becoming Jeffers'
perishing republic all set to vanish in one final blast with
the rest of a despairing world
America
you seem bent on taking that world along with you just for

the ride
America
phoney as a Hollywood cowboy main street, laughable as
  Rockefeller with his ten-cent pieces, vulgar as a Las Vegas
  night club, brave as your airmen machine-gunning river-
  front refugees in broad daylight of Dresden's holocaust
America
you have learned from everyone's history but your own
America
all the Kennedys left cannot help you now
America
I've learned how you operate, I know how votes are managed,
  who has his coat pockets stuffed with bribes, who finds
  himself asked to be Assistant Secretary of this or that,
  who is tossed out finally with nothing left but bitterness
  eating at his heart
America
you kept Pound locked up all those years — he had you
  pegged, Usura, he had you dead to rights, betrayers of
  Jefferson, he had you figured out good so you left him
  caged and cooking in the sun at Pisa hoping to drive him
  mad — but he put the record straight about Roosevelt,
  you hoped to bury him but instead he walks a free man
  now, his vision haunting you with its signature of doom
America
was promises nobody has kept or ever intended keeping
America
how do you turn quiet home-loving men in five short years
  into hate-fired Black Muslim avengers who write and
  scream out to their brothers: break doors, smash windows
  at night or anytime, bust in every store window, drag out
  all you can carry, set fire, kill or maim whitey, pump holes
  in every dirty cop or get him good with a brick or your
  own two hands
America
give it all back to the Indians if they can stand the smell
  and the flies around the corpse
America
how easily your myths tarnish, how expendable are your
  heroes, how quickly, how easily you swallow good people

into your patented garbage disposal, then grind them down
into nice little pieces to be carted away to the dump with
the same care accorded the ashes of dead Japanese soldiers
(but none the less garbage, waste products of your restless
unsatisfied ambition hanging like a cancer cloud, a plague
of slowly spreading death over the world)
America
you have been tested and found wanting
America
the world has watched you in Vietnam and even its hardened
stomach has been turned, you have all but buried yourself
in your own Coca-Cola beer can litter, your bar-to-bar
Saigon filth so well aped by the small men you came to
save but instead have corrupted forever; after your crazy
"weed killer" squadrons have bared all the trees, after
your Incinderjell has roasted all available corpses, then
perhaps we'll see at last every barbed wire death camp,
count every tin can house left standing, see how much
rice still grows — after the last plane has been shot down
out of the sky we'll be able to see who owns all the graft
concessions now, who hands out the government pay-offs
and who opens unnumbered bank accounts in Switzerland
daily — but until then we watch as your Marines advance,
as the underground bunkers are cooked out one by one,
as the aircraft let go their terror bombs hoping these latest
villages have a few more V.C. than the ones raided yesterday — the whole world watches, wonders how it will end,
while you twine yourself more and more with the dragon
coils of your own premeditated meddling
America
America
there is really nothing left to do now but die with a certain
gracefulness
really nothing left to do
America
in the name of God you never trusted, e pluribus unum

February, 1968

Epilogue

America

tonight fiery candles of the black man's mass burn crimson
  in the skies of Washington, Chicago, tributes from the
  ghettos to your Gandhi struck down by bullet of hate, the
  Gun used again to work out history, the Gun in the hands
  of the lawless once again making jungles of your streets,
  mockery of your laws, the Gun that gave you birth, that
  burned on its red-hot gun barrel flesh of brother turned
  against brother, once again supreme — so wheel out machine guns, unsling the shotguns, line up the sights from
  the armoured car, shoot to kill, shoot to kill, shoot to kill,
  kill, kill, kill

America

April 5, 1968

The Folger Factor in Canadian-American Relationships

Arnold Edinborough

The Folger Shakespeare Library in Washington, D.C. is not representative of anything in the United States. But it was the first place I ever went to outside of Canada, and I there met with enough different people and enough different attitudes to know that all my stereotypes about what I still called America, learned in England and Canada, were wrong.

Through the Judge Hardy films, I knew all American teenagers were bobby-soxed swingers who drove cars and had unlimited pocket money. The curator's children weren't, didn't, and hadn't.

From my colleagues in the English Department at Queen's University, I knew that all American scholars were Germanic in their erudition, literal in their interpretations, and concerned with publication only lest they perish. Around the tea table (tea!) every afternoon all the research-readers in the library met to chat about their work. The talk was as good as in any faculty club in Canada (we didn't have a faculty club at Queen's), the attitudes a good deal more humane, and the people a great deal better-informed. There were historians reading plays, one law professor reading history, myself immersed in documents about the Royal Wardrobe of Henry VIII, and an ex-Marine captain in the process of inventing a collating machine.

The director of the library was from North Carolina and drove a Cadillac. Not because of his salary but because when he had graduated in 1930, he had won two $100 prizes which he had invested in Borden's and Coca-Cola. "Even in a depression," he said, "I figured Americans would always drink pop and eat ice cream." His stock, bought at rock-bottom prices, had been split so often he'd stopped counting. He drove a Cadillac just on the interest.

I also knew that every American said "drop in some time," but none ever asked you to a given place at a specific time. The director, the curator, the chief cataloguer, and the senior research fellow, however, all asked me to dinner or took me to lunch. I still correspond with three or four twenty years later and thirteen years after I resigned from university teaching.

And I was in Washington: soul-less capital of a materialistic nation. Yet it was difficult to concentrate on the Folger and its unbelievable research resources when the best collection of Italian Renaissance art outside Italy was only six blocks from my hotel; when the Smithsonian, that national attic full of surprises, was opposite the National Gallery; when the floodlit public buildings were a delight to walk amongst on hot summer nights; and when the living historical tradition of South versus North was all around you or within an hour's drive.

I found then that the cultivated American is a delight to talk to and that the cultural resources of his country are enormous. I found that all my stereotypes were wrong (as they should be) and that whenever I think of the Americans as loudmouthed, brash, master-racist bullies, I try to think of the people I actually knew (and know) in Washington.

Two phrases then come back to me. One is written round the statue of Puck in the gardens of the Folger Library — "Oh, what fools these mortals be" — and I think how foolish the American politicians are to ignore the real resources of their nation. The other was said often by the girl in the Reading Room. When you thanked her for bringing up another six boxes of dusty documents or for lugging enormous folios to your table, she would smile and say, "Why, you're entirely welcome."

It is that phrase, that voice, and that attitude which keep me hopeful about what is now the most powerful nation on earth. It even modifies that anti-Americanism which is only skin-deep in any Canadian living next door — including me.

1966

C. J. Newman

America you bastard
murderer of dreams
(and dreams are your
most innocent murders)
seed-blaster
harvest-ghoul

Fortress America! If only
the fortress walls were real
and high enough
to spare us having to watch
your long dark night of the soul
your reaching out for that murder
that one more murder
final murder
to purge you of murder
and of all experience
— if only

Seed-blaster
harvest-ghoul
are you finally choked
on the fat of your land
and have you run out of your own poor
to shit upon and are you ready
now to burst out
— the half-digested riches
of the earth

exploding from your every pore
to infect us all

America America
the burnt seed lies by the side
of your turnpikes
auto graveyards
motel cities
military camps
the heaped-up contempt
of every dream of paradise on earth
stinking your greens
the burnt seed
shines darkly
blasting out
the sun

Centennial Song

Robin Mathews

Canada, my beauty,
everybody's love,
white flower of the diamond-studded North,
let me tell you that
a tired prostitute beyond her prime,
dejected, hungry,
full of malice and uncertain fear
would throw her charms away less openly,
would exercise more choice
than you have ever done,
would charge at least a reasonable rate,
would try to be
(within the perils of the trade)
a self-respecting whore;
And What Is More
even in her wildest state
of drunken self-delusion,
howling at a corner
where the newsies thrive,
she wouldn't let you see her
stopping people —
friends and neighbours,
even relatives,
shouting with paranoid insistence
upon decency and moral strength,
that she is living better now than ever,
friends with everyone, and that
despite all rumour, not a shred
of proof has ever been produced
to show that she
(as gossips say)
is being regularly screwed.

Various Americas

George Woodcock

I am a Canadian, and a birthright one, in spite of the unin-
formed xenophobe who recently, in an issue of *Canadian
Dimension*, denounced me as a "former Englishman." When
I try to set out the reasons why I take pleasure in this fact,
I find myself at first evoking eloquent vaguenesses. The land
attracts me, of course; I feel a swell of emotion coasting in
over the great muddy fan of the Fraser from Japan with the
mountains rimming the horizon, or sailing up the St. Law-
rence with the northern lights pulsating over the starboard
sky. I know of no city, among the hundreds I have passed
through or lived in in Europe, Asia, Africa, and the Americas,
which I would sooner make my place of constant return than
Vancouver, whose combination of sea, mountain, and pearly
light seems to me inimitable. And as I look forward to the
day, a week ahead, when I shall start on a long meandering
drive across the country from Pacific to Atlantic, I feel a
habitual excitement mounting at the prospect of those prodi-
gal vastnesses — mountains — then plains — then lakes, all
enough for a dozen normal lands — and the great river at
the end, duplicating the great river at the beginning, with
Montreal as a crown of human vitality and blessed with
dozen-landed disunity.

But what else do I like about being a Canadian? I am
nonplussed for an answer, searching among the nebulosities
of our national life, until I think of America, as we allow the
citizens of the United States to name their fragments of the
continent. Then points appear in the greyness, lines and
lineaments coalesce; I realize that, apart from the mere
physical features of landscape and climate, apart from a
handful of painters and fewer writers, what I like enough

about Canada to make me prefer it to so many other countries are precisely the points at which it differs — and shows at least a chance of continuing to differ — from the giant to the south.

Let me make it clear. I am not saying that everything in Canada is superior; in many areas we are obviously a great deal less advanced or less accomplished than some Americans. Nor am I a Canadian nationalist, for I detest nationalism of every kind, though I think there are loyalites to one's setting and one's culture which are beneficial as long as they do not imply a willingness to comfort Everyman's Enemy — the monstrous regiment of politicians and bureaucrats. At the same time I am not, except in moments of wild talk, anti-American. I like Americans at home, though I find that, like most other people, they often show up badly as travellers. I have a deep, nostalgic affection for American places. I publish with American publishers, and there are American magazines to which I am proud to contribute. Melville and Thoreau and James are as much in my spiritual ancestry as Tolstoy and Li Po (which incidentally is why I cannot be anti-Russian or anti-Chinese either). I recognize the presence in American history of a populist tradition of the most gallant kind, a tradition which has been sustained in our day by Americans like A. J. Muste and Paul Goodman, and I know that those who follow it are inspired by the libertarian concepts which have exercised a varying but never absent influence on my own life and work since the 1930's.

Yet in the world of the 1960's, I would rather be a Canadian than an American, and there are certain forms of American influence over Canada which I regard with as much apprehension as the most rabid of the young Canadian nationalists. The reason why I fear and dislike America *as a political entity* is that, by a combination of historical circumstances and constitutional errors, it has become far more menacing to its own people and to the outer world than Canada can or will ever be. America's strengths *as a state* are its gravest flaws; Canada's weaknesses *as a state* are its greatest virtues.

As a libertarian, I am distrustful of any but the most light and provisional of political systems. Since anarchy is unlikely to come in my lifetime or for many generations, I prefer among existing patterns those of a most pronouncedly cantonal character, with the maximum of decentralization and direct democracy; I would like every country to be a union of the Appenzells. That is why I find no terrors in what is being said in Quebec; I would welcome more than anything else Canada's cantonalization into any number of associate states, provinces, free cities, or whatever we might care to call them, with, since we can fortunately never aspire to be a great power and therefore do not need the apparatus proper to such a monstrosity, the slightest of coordinating councils at the top.

But even such a liberated political structure, with which Canada might initiate a new political era in the world, seems remote indeed while we have leaders obsessed with the vanities of directing a strong and centralized state. And in considering things as they are, we have to compare what actually exists: an American system based on executive authority and irresponsibility on the one hand, and a Canadian system of responsible parliamentary government on the other.

The American system was devised by revolutionary idealists impressed by the utopian visions of the Enlightenment; it was not a slow and organic growth like English parliamentarianism, but the product of abstract planning. The founding fathers had the best of good intentions, and it was with the thought of safeguarding liberty that they devised an unrealistic triad of separated executive, legislative, and judicial functions. In practice, the protective barriers became the bars of freedom's prison; more than a hundred years ago the first great Anglo-Saxon conscript armies were raised in the "sweet land of liberty" to shed their blood in the meaningless slaughter of the Civil War; just forty years ago Sacco and Vanzetti were only the most famous of those who died unjustly for demanding in its logical extremity the freedom which the Constitution was meant to guarantee; for every Canadian Riel there have been dozens of American Joe Hills, killed or tortured by men who believed they were defending what the American Revolution was fought to achieve.

The legislative pattern of the United States in some way parallels the Swiss cantonal system; it has the same dual chambers, based on representation by population in the House and on equal representation for each state in the Senate. But the Americans never added the saving Swiss devices of referendum and initiative, by which the people can take back, when necessary, much of the power they have delegated. Also, as the United States has developed over the past 180 years, the effect of the Senate has been not to safeguard the interests of the weaker regions — its original intent — but to create a conservative stranglehold by giving backward, low-population areas more influence over national policies than progressive urban regions. Canada's Senate is probably as hospitable a stable for dinosaurs as America's, but our dinosaurs are safely fossilized, whereas in Washington Tyrannosaurus Rex still ramps in all his grisly Southern vigour.

But real power in the United States, probably since Lincoln and certainly since Roosevelt, has increasingly gravitated away from the legislative bodies and the Supreme Court, which flashes sporadic light into the pervading Washington darkness, and towards an executive which is not responsible to the legislature and which, no matter what its blunders, cannot be voted out of office until the end of its four years' incumbency. Four American presidents have been assassinated; none has ever been put out of the way by a vote of No Confidence. The American president may live in danger physically, but politically he is far less vulnerable than any parliamentary prime minister; he also has far greater powers. Theoretically democratic, the American executive system is in practice strictly authoritarian, which is why a strong president irrevocably marks and names, like a monarch, the era he dominates. An American president in fact resembles a parliamentary leader far less than he resembles the tyrants of ancient Greece, men put into power by the people to get rid of the kings, but granted vast and almost kingly authority, which inevitably they used to perpetuate their rule and strengthen their hold on the land.

But the presidency does not stand alone. As its power has increased during the present century, it has nurtured under its aegis a whole group of monolithic and repressive executive institutions (Pentagon, CIA, FBI, etc.) which are in no real way controlled by Congress and which carry on from president to president so that the authoritarian chain is never broken, no matter how the party allegiance of the president himself may change.

The pattern of authority which originated in mistaken idealism has been nurtured by misapplied righteousness. As I. F. Stone declared at the great Washington rally against the Vietnam War in April, 1965, "the men directing America's cruel policies are decent human beings like you and me, caught up in monstrous institutions that have a life of their own." These institutions have come into being largely because of the tendency to cumulative growth which is inherent in all authoritarian bureaucratic institutions. But they have also been fostered by the necessities of the role which the United States has accepted, that of executor of deceased empires and censor of the world's political morals. Only a great power with immense resources can attempt such a task, but in assuming it the United States has incurred an ironic consequence, that of becoming itself one of the three great existing world empires and of embarking on a war in Vietnam which is morally as devastating as any war fought by cynical power maniacs.

The sense of being held powerless under the weight of a monolithic authoritarian structure underlies many of the dramatic disturbances in America today. There is a Dead Sea quality about even the gifts of such a system. The morning after the euphoria of the great civil rights movement, with its triumphs that have been largely meaningless in terms of real human elevation, set the mood for the great Negro summer riots. Disillusionment with impersonal, computerized education, with do-good programs that merely create permanent lumpenproletariats, with the new affluence that demands conformity, have helped as much as Vietnam and the draft to create an anarchic, resentful mood among the best of the young, whether activist New Lefters or passivist hippies.

Canada's parliamentary system, where the prime minister and his cabinet are in perpetual political danger, particularly in the fortunate days of minority government, has saved us from the development of vast political father figures and of irresponsible and all-powerful executive agencies like those which today disfigure American government. We have no generals dictating policy because we are lucky enough to have no hope of and no taste for becoming militarily powerful. We have no CIA. And, though reactionary statements by Canadian police bosses leave no doubt of their authoritarian longings, they are not yet in control of us; the RCMP is not yet the FBI, though at times it runs as its jackal. Both Canadians and Americans realize the difference. Few Quebeckers, whatever they may say, really feel, as so many American Negroes do, that there is no way out but violence. And, with a sure instinct, Americans are countering the famous brain-drain southward with a conscience-drain northward, many of their young men emigrating every day to a land where conscription is not a permanent institution and where, for the moment, the political air is a little cleaner and somewhat easier to breathe.

The American monolith being what it is, we who live under its shadow at noon cannot ignore it. Economically and culturally, the flow goes on between the two countries, whatever their political differences, and that is inevitable. What is not inevitable is the political satellitism into which a fatalistic view of being neighbours to a colossus has led our politicians. Many Canadians are concerned because our industries are dominated by American capital, because our air waves are choked with the products of American radio and television, because our bookstalls are loaded with American magazines and paperbacks. I agree that there is reason for concern here, but less than there is in our unwillingness to throw off the sycophantic attitude towards American policies which our governments have forced on us for the past quarter of a century. There is a stubborn myth that an American alliance is necessary for our safety in a world where war always threatens. In fact, we should recognize before it is too late that American politicians have never considered Canada more than the expandable screen, the outer rampart, which might absorb the first wave of an attack. The interests of Canada have been their last concern, but they should be our first concern; it is time we realized that military alliances with aggressive powers always lead to peril and that in the world's eyes we are damned for the crimes of our associates even when we do not take part in them.

It is high time we asserted our moral independence, and for that assertion two acts seem today indispensable. We must take the logical stand of an independent country with nothing to gain by war in a world of nuclear fission and declare our neutrality, denouncing both NORAD and NATO. To make sure that our neutrality and our dissociation from American policies are understood, we should declare in unequivocal tones the disgust which most Canadians feel for the war in Vietnam. Only after such a clear statement of independence has been made should we turn to such tasks as the more intensive fostering of our native culture and the decision as to whether we can build an autonomous economy.

Such assertions of independence would promote in the long run a healthier and more realistic relationship between Canada and the United States than has existed for many years. They might even have profound effects within America and encourage those who seek liberation from the country's present evils. For, even in rejecting the monstrousness of the American power structure, we must never turn away from that other America, fraternal to all the world, which endures suffering and discrimination in its stand for the populist and libertarian values official America has forgotten. Thoreau, after all, was an American, and perhaps he represents the deepest-running of all American strains.

O Canada

Louis Dudek

Who owns Canada? You know who owns Canada
to the extent of 26,000,000,000 cash
    (How much do you think the place is worth?)
increasing at the rate of one billion a year —
perishable imports
    paid for with natural resources.

By the time we reach One World
    we'll already have been one Continent.
There are short cuts to the future.

If Throughout His Reign Napoleon . . .

Stephen Vizinczey

In her masterpiece on the Vietnam mystery, Mary McCarthy describes a fascinating psychological phenomenon of dissociation. "The American," she writes, "is pictured as completely sundered from his precision weaponry as if he had no control over it, in the same way as Johnson, escalating, feigns to have no option in the war and to react like an automat to moves from Hanoi." "Feigns," though, isn't the verb. The protestations of powerlessness to step outside the power struggle over Vietnam (uttered in tones of dignified detachment by men who are so passionately involved that their nerves no longer react to the horrors they inflict), the professions of sympathy and concern, are too glaringly contradictory and incongruous to be considered a cynical and therefore rational attempt to quell public indignation.

The stance of sorrowing innocence appears to me just as compulsive as the burning of Vietnam. Every obsession carries its tail end of reverse feeling: whether it concerns the extermination of the race or the pursuit of a woman beyond reach or the subjugation of the little brown Reds, or whatever absurdity, when the victim is no longer able to control his involvement, then he needs at least the illusion that he is still in charge of himself; and the greater the obsession, the more compelling is the need for unrelated or opposite feelings to allow one a sense of freedom despite one's enslavement. The alcoholic on all fours insists that though he drinks he is always sober; he drinks, in fact, only to be able to think straight — he wouldn't touch the stuff if it made him drunk. The American language has the apt phrase: genuine phoney.

There are many explanations for the hawks' obsession with Vietnam, and most of them are valid at some level. The hypothesis I'd like to advance, nonetheless, is that this obsession originates in a deeper, more personal and intense feeling than the fear of China, of abandoning Southeast Asia to communism, or of losing face and elections. It originates in the frustrating, maddening pursuit of the unattainable — power. The truth is that power (in the sense individuals long for it) is a mirage. And it is in the pursuit of mirages that people lose their minds.

"Power is a word the meaning of which we do not understand," wrote Tolstoy, whose concluding essay in *War and Peace* has lost none of its relevance:

> If throughout his reign Napoleon continues to issue commands concerning the invasion of England and expends on no other undertaking so much time and effort, and yet during his whole reign never once attempts to execute his design but undertakes an expedition to Russia, with which country, according to his repeatedly expressed conviction, he considers it to his advantage to be in alliance — then this results from the fact that his commands did not correspond to the course of events in the first case but did so in the latter.
>
> For the command to be carried out to the letter it must be a command actually capable of fulfillment. But to know what can and what cannot be carried out is impossible, not only in the case of Napoleon's invasion of Russia, in which millions participated, but even in the case of the simplest event, seeing that both the one and the other are liable at any moment to find themselves confronted by millions of obstacles. Every command executed is always one of an immense number unexecuted. All commands inconsistent with the course of events are impossible and do not get carried out. Only the possible ones link up into a consecutive series of commands corresponding to a series of events, and are carried out. (Rosemary Edmond's translation)

No wonder that Johnson can talk with such feeling about "the limitations of even the most powerful nation" and tell his critics "we cannot do everything we want." Such statements may appear refreshingly pragmatic in comparison with harangues from Peking, but even speaking of "limitations" is twisting a painful truth to fit a delusion. Far from being in the enviable position of lacking the means to do everything they want in the world, they cannot be certain of their ability to achieve *any* of their aims.

Politics is indeed the art of the possible, except that one can only guess what is possible. If throughout his reign Napoleon issued commands which were to lead to the invasion of England, yet invaded Russia instead, if the Soviet and American leaders acted in 1956 to establish a lasting peace and increase their own influence in the Middle East, if Nasser closed the Straits of Tiran to weaken Israel, if successive American presidents have issued orders designed to bring peace, stability, and security to Vietnam — then it must be concluded that when a man wields power he has little notion of what he is actually doing. Not because he is necessarily more stupid than we are, but because his authority relates him to such an immense number of possibilities: events that may or may not occur will cancel out his commands or thwart their execution or alter their effect or, sometimes (and this is the tantalizing part of it), permit them to be carried out.

To have power is to experience chaos, the core of human existence — which creates such a deep sense of uncertainty, such an abiding conviction that anything is possible, that the men around Kennedy, some of the best-informed men in the country, could leap to the conclusion that the assassination was part of a communist conspiracy to take over the United States. The "limitation" of power is that it is a nightmare.

The traditional Eastern response to the chaos of life has been inertia; the traditional Western reaction has been to ignore the nature of life (the flux of billions of laws and occurrences) and to behave as if we could impose our will upon events, as if we could command the future. Taking chances, we were bound to be lucky now and then, if in limited ways; and indeed it is worthwhile to challenge the multitude of contingencies so that the right one *may* occur. But to keep one's sanity one must never lose sight of the fact that one can only try. We must, in Camus' phrase, "act without faith." If events do not echo to our cry of command, we must give up, for no power on earth can create a single occurrence that is not already a potent possibility.

The inability of men of power not only to create new realities but even to impose the image of something that doesn't exist (as opposed to mirages like American or Arab invincibility, which are generated by social and psychological needs) was analyzed by Hannah Arendt in her essay "Truth and Politics." Despite the all-pervasive mass media at their command, she observes, the newsmanagers achieve the opposite of their intention: the result of their unremitting efforts is that people won't believe even the time of day. "The consistent lying, metaphorically speaking, pulls the ground from under our feet and provides no other ground on which to stand." The powerful can destroy the truth, but they cannot replace it.

Though it is impossible to create the image of a Vietnam that doesn't exist, let alone bring forth an actual country that isn't there, Johnson and his colleagues are bent on producing a democratic (Western) or at least a friendly, reliable South Vietnam. As they pursue policies based on the decisive and independent efficacy of power — a force in history which is wholly imaginary — they are increasingly losing touch with reality and suffer the intellectual and emotional consequences. (And this is the phenomenon that Lord Acton, witty and dead wrong, defined as "absolute power corrupts absolutely" — an observation which made Stalin laugh bitterly in one of his sane moments. Camus was nearer the truth in *Caligula*: it is because the emperor cannot have the moon that he takes leave of his senses.)

Hubris is evidently the mental epidemic of our age, and its germ is the universal daydream that whatever we really, intensely believe to be right and wish and work for, must and will happen. In fact, most people would shake their heads over an individual who behaved as if he expected his life to take this happy course, but many of the same people somehow assume that the rules of life change for the benefit of a class or a nation, whose collective destiny unfurls as a huge colour TV spectacular with the right flags filling the screen at the end.

Americans, in particular, still seem to be paying the price for the glory of World War II. They willed to win, they had right and might on their side, they killed and died for victory; how then could they see that all this had but a very tenuous connection with the outcome? The whole show seems so easy to repeat. The British were brought down (or at least closer) to earth by the immediate dissolution of their Empire, but the Americans acquired one with less time and effort than they are now expending on the Viet Cong. In history nothing fails like success because it tempts nations to take their good luck for the measure of their strength.

And then there is the notion that, with everything else, power has "progressed" — that the totalitarian features of society, industrial wealth, superior weapons have made power grow, that it has become more effective than it used to be. But improvements in armaments, communications, technology, do not change the nature of power, which is potent only when it corresponds to the course of events. Having more of the same unreal thing doesn't make it any more real. Power is still a stick and then the mirage of a stick; now you have it, now you don't; when you have it, it may be a bigger stick — but when you don't, it's just a bigger mirage.

To understand this would be to realize that we can trust God to help those who help themselves only because he likes to play mean practical jokes.

To withdraw from Vietnam, Johnson would have to come to disbelieve in, and be willing to explode, the myth of power and thus the myth of the United States as "the most powerful nation the world has ever seen." But how could Johnson shed the delusion of his nation when most of his critics share it? They tell him that he should use the immense power of his office for better purposes! So this great might that everybody is talking about must exist somewhere; it must materialize with a few more soldiers, social workers, ambassadors, bombs. But while none of these can turn a single Vietnamese into a democrat, the bombs do go off and thereby strengthen the illusion that if one can destroy the world, one must also be able to control it. So he just can't let go. This is the psychology of escalation.

The war in Vietnam is a fight to the death to prove that man can do what he wills. Given the absurdity of its premise, this little war could destroy the United States even without the introduction of nuclear weapons. To avoid the brief humiliation of withdrawal and its repercussions, the U.S. government settles for demonstrating year after year its inability to subdue a rebellious little nation; and the war which has been fought to prevent a chain reaction in Laos and Cambodia has already produced a chain reaction, as commentators have noted, in Newark and Detroit.

It seems, then, that the American president has no reasonable alternative but to stop trying to create events that are not possibilities, realities that do not exist, and dare his people to face the facts of life.

"My fellow Americans," he might inconceivably say, "I may be the most powerful man in history, but in fact I don't have the power to carry through all the social and economic changes necessary to transform the slums within a five-mile radius of the White House.

"I could try harder, and I might or might not succeed — there are too many imponderables. Remember Prohibition? I couldn't be absolutely certain of success even if I abolished Congress and you accepted me as dictator with the combined prerogatives of Alexander the Great, Napoleon, Stalin, and Hitler, with a thousand big computers and all the intellectuals working out the details. The only thing certain is that I couldn't make the Negroes more equal than the rest of you could be inspired to tolerate them to be. Now, as to our efforts to build a new society in the southern part of Vietnam . . . .

"As you know, we were fighting there not just on account of that piece of jungle but because we didn't want to hand over the control of Southeast Asia to the communists. However, I made a shocking discovery. There is no such thing as control over Southeast Asia. Mao nearly started another revolution just to get hold of the control over China, which gave him the slip the first time around, but it seems this dragon doesn't exist either. So I'm giving him one more mirage to pursue; let him and his successors go stark raving mad over it."

But there is, of course, the gun. The only thing real and solid among the floating clouds of possibilities. The guns, the ships, the planes, the bombs, the missiles, the Bomb. The cruelties of power are the rage of impotence.

Billboards Build Freedom of Choice

Earle Birney

(billboard on Oregon coastal highway)

Yegitit?
Look see
        AMERICA BUILDS BILLBOARDS
so billboards kin bill freedoma choice
between — yeah between billbores no
        WAIT
its yedoan hafta choose no more between
say like trees and billbores lessa course
wenna buncha trees is flattint out inta
        BILLB—
yeah yegotit
youkin pick between well
hey!   see!   like dat!
        ALL VINYL GET WELL DOLLS $6.98
or — watch wasdat comin up?
        PRE PAID CAT?
        PREPAID CATASTROPHE COVERAGE
yeah hell youkin have damnear anythin
        FREE 48 INCH TV IN EVERY ROOM
see!   or   watchit!
        OUR PIES TASTE LIKE MOTHERS
yeah but look bud no chickenin out
because billbores build
        AM—
yeah an AMERICA BUILDS MORE
buildbores to bill more —
sure yugotta! yugotta have
        FREEDOM TO
hey! you doan wannem godam fieldglasses!
theys probly clouds on Mount Raneer

but not on
> *MOUNT RAINIER THE BEER THAT CHEERS*

and not on good old yella
> SHELL

keepin de windoff yuh from allose clammy
beaches *hey!*
> LOOK

yewan cows? Zooooom! Them was
> BORDEN'S CONTENTED

Landscapes is for the birds fella
yegotta choose between well like
between two a de same
hell like de man said Who's got time
for a third tit? *Two* parties is *Okay*
that's DEMOC sure but yegit three
yegot COMMIES I'm tellinyeh
is like dose damfool niggers in
in Asia someweres all tryin to be nootrul
I tellyeh treesa crowd   a crowda
godamatheisticunamericananti
> BILLBORES

yeah an yewanna help Burma?   help
> *BURMA SHAVE*

yewanna keep the longhairs from starvin?
> BUY HANDMADE TOY SOLDIERS

yegotta choose fella yegotta
choose between
> AMERICA and UN—

between KEE-RISPIES and KEE-RUMPIES
between KEE-RYEST and KEEROOST-SHOVE
and brother if you doan pick
> RIGHT

you better
git this heap
tahelloffn
our
> TRUWAY

I Love Americans

Hugh Garner

I like the U.S.A. and the American people.

My first visit to the United States was as an unemployed migratory worker in the early '30's, when I crossed the Rainbow Bridge at Niagara Falls with a nickel toll in my pocket. After waiting for a half hour or so for my chum to cross (he had the other nickel from the dime he had scrounged before we hitchhiked out of Toronto), I went on alone, subsequently learning that he had been turned back.

My first lift, on a narrow highway running towards Rochester, N.Y., was with an American Indian woman driving a beat-up old coupe with a rumble seat. She drove me to the outskirts of Rochester. There I was picked up by four teen-age youths who bought a basket of plums, which they called "prunes," and I must have eaten half of the basket, for it was the first food I'd had all day.

My introduction to the U.S.A. was not an auspicious one by any means, but from my first day in the United States, I have always been treated well by the Americans, and over the years since I have grown to look upon them not as cousins who speak my language but, almost, as my own people. For parts of several years I worked as a bus boy and handbill deliverer in New York and have lived there on transient relief, in the city's rooming houses, and later in its hotels. I have beaten my way from Boston to Los Angeles on freight trains, picked tomatoes near Santa Barbara, California, found a dollar bill beside the Illinois Central tracks near Yazoo City, Mississippi (one of two dollars cash I had all that winter), and slept on a bench in the Endicott-Johnson shoe company locker room in Endicott, N.Y.

As a Canadian I carry a big inferiority complex with me

when I visit the United States, as I do two or three times every summer. This despite the fact that I drive new cars, have a wallet full of credit cards and cash in my pocket. This national inferiority complex is a debilitating factor in Canadian life and, I suspect, the *raison d'être* of this collection. An analogy closer to home is the parochial and provincial attitude of Maritimers towards the wealthier, more sophisticated citizens of "Upper Canada," particularly those who live in Ontario. It is a dislike founded on jealousy and envy.

There are facets of American life that I do not agree with, the Vietnam War as a current example, and a decade or so ago the paranoia connected with the rise of McCarthyism in Congress. Pitted against these flaws, however, are the good things about the U.S.A. and Americans: their generosity, their friendliness, their overwhelming love of life. This generosity and friendliness is an impossible goal for the average Canadian to emulate, for it needs a base of self-confidence and self-knowledge that comes from knowing you are the wealthiest and biggest. An example here would be the Calvinistic attitude of the Scots towards the English.

My people, the English, formed the second immigrant group to the shores of what is now the United States of America (after the Spanish), and it was they or their descendants, who had settled Massachusetts and Virginia, who revolted against King George III. They not only brought to America their sense of fair play, their inherent radicalism, and their foreknowledge of their destiny, but also such attributes of the English, up to and including the First World War, as come from being citizens of a strong, powerful nation. It was Canada's misfortune to be settled, in its Anglo-Saxon-Celt sections, by Scots Highlanders, who have bequeathed to us their dour Presbyterian attitude towards not only sin but towards drinking, fornicating, gambling, and even living itself.

As Canadians we feel pretty smug about our lack of a colour problem and tend to forget that Canada too had slaves before the British abolition of slavery by Wilberforce. The Negro in Canada is still a second-class citizen, though his dearth of numbers forces him to accept the fact.

The recent confrontation between white and black in the United States is a tragic thing, more tragic for the Negro than for whitey, but a tragedy for them both. Unlike some of the hotshot "freedom marchers" from Canada who performed the gesture of going into the American South to interfere with the Negro struggle for basic human rights, I have stayed clear of personal involvement in a situation that belongs to the U.S.A. alone. I see no amelioration of the Negro problem in the United States at the present time, and I can understand the white backlash, just as I can understand the Anglo-Saxon backlash here that is developing against the French-Canadians in Quebec. I think it is unfair and unrealistic that ten per cent of the American public, because of the colour of its skin, is denied the full benefits of American citizenship, but the current white American ninety per cent didn't bring the Negro to America; it was their forefathers and our forefathers, the English settlers and planters. As a foreigner I must leave the settlement of the American Negro problem to the Americans, in the full knowledge that there are intelligent and dedicated men, both black and white, in the United States who are working to bring it to a just and honourable conclusion.

I think the Americans are an intrinsically good people, despite their use of napalm against Vietnamese villagers, their paranoiac attitude towards communism, and their muscular interference in the Dominican Republic. I served in the Spanish Civil War in the original American battalion, the Abraham Lincoln, and I came to know and admire the Americans as fighting men and as overly generous friends of the Spanish people.

The Americans today are not the Americans of the McCarthy period, nor are they the Americans of World War Two or the depression. The United States is not a static country but moves forward in waves, sometimes radical, sometimes reactionary, but always moving forward as the world's most powerful nation.

In the process of becoming the most powerful force for both good and evil in the world today, they have made many enemies and will continue to do so. As an Englishman born just prior to the First World War, I can understand this. When I was born, England, consisting of the United Kingdom but generally referred to as England alone, was the most powerful and arrogant nation on earth. She made a host of enemies, and some of these enmities have not yet died. Were I an American, I too would be puzzled by the hatreds stirred up among the very people — the Arab block, for instance — that I had helped so generously in the past, but as an Englishman I could afford to ignore these hostilities.

Since I was six years old I have lived in a country that is a northern annex to the world's most powerful state, and my attitude towards it is coloured not only by propinquity but also by comparison. Despite their sometime faults and the arrogance that comes from financial and muscular strength, I like and admire the American people. My box score to date as both a hobo and a car-driving tourist is thirty-eight of the continental United States, and in a couple of weeks my wife and I hope to raise this by visiting some northwestern states we have yet to see. We will drive out there secure in the knowledge that we are among friends who speak our language, are friendly and generous towards us, and will make us feel at home. What more could we ask?

State of *The Nation*

Peter Stevens

(April 24, 1967)
All good Americans can see
what dogs those Commies are,
to abuse a good-natured man like Hubert,
who comes to them
with a big grin on his face,
love in his heart,
and just a whiff
of napalm.

Balancing the Books

Jack Ludwig

Handle what I say with care.

I'm a Canadian, but I've lived in the U.S.A. among Americans for a long time now. At this moment I'm living in London (should I add, *not* our Canadian London?), and this British-subjected, American-residenced, Canadian-citizened guy hears the anti-American pitches of dying, dead, and not-yet-born men, women, and countries.

Nobody likes someone else's power.

Nobody could possibly like Lyndon Johnson.

Nobody could possibly believe in a theory which says Dean Rusk is animate.

Nobody could ignore the part in McNamara's hair or the glint of his glasses.

Nobody can hear Westmoreland talk about Vietnam with the military cliché of "real estate," or hear his men say they have to get them one "Victor Charlie," without being aware that the American killer-boy scout is one of the more brutal dangers to be unleashed on this sad, sad world.

Nobody can watch the consequences of Johnson's Vietnam policy without seeing America torn apart with deep rents which will not be repaired for one or even two generations.

There has always been a bully element in the United States: the glorification of the tough Marine and the first-line defenders against the onslaughts of communism stuff has removed shade and colouring from the military and political world view of official America: the real world is now assumed to be what the armed forces' code of conduct pamphlet says it is: the pop art, comic strip view of the AOK gee-whizzer is now a photograph.

Nobody can pass through Russia as I did recently without knowing that the Vietnam War is the greatest boon to the U.S.S.R. since Sputnik, that never in a million years of planning and putting out with Moscow gold could the Soviets have come up with something so divisive, so dramatically revealing of all the hardnesses and uglinesses of the military-industrialist power group in America. While there is a Vietnam there is, eventually, an end to the relevance of Siniavsky and Daniel, to the Russian *michin malicho* in the Middle East, the oppression in the surrounding Eastern European countries, the nasty attitudes towards religious Jews: Vietnam is the big BUT. Without it millions of people in Eastern Europe might ask themselves, "How are we doing?"

So Johnson and Rusk aren't merely blind. They're dumb.

The country's balance of payments and gold drain fix is a direct result of Vietnam. Cities will be ripped apart. Research will be abandoned. More and more men and money will go into Operation Rat-hole, dwarfing all others. The bright young people who might save this stupid government will be permanently turned-off by government and political involvements. A stick of grass is better than a cycle of Cathay or an acre of Middlesex.

And think what would happen if the loonies who are pushing Johnson on to greater and greater absurdities were actually able to make America *win*! All that money and blood and agony for what couldn't be traded in for two tickets to the Dempsey-Firpo fight!

Dear friends: America is the country where I, among others, have said in print these very same things I say here, and one of the people who has consistently argued for my right to do so is Robert McNamara. Lyndon Johnson, who is now probably past praying for, pushed through the only civil rights legislation worth remembering. What *should* we make of that?

America is a country of kooks. America is capable of coming to its senses.

Think of them this way:

Richard Nixon is an American, but so is Robert Lowell.

Lyndon Johnson is an American politician, but so is Gene McCarthy.

The DAR is an American organization, but so is the New York *Times*, not just the newspaper which daily opposes the administration on Vietnam and a dozen other crucial issues, but the billboard on which one sees posted a thousand concerts, a hundred plays, a hundred poetry readings, and a fantastic number of significant first-class artistic and cultural events which sit side by side with the DAR and a hundred other know-nothing, philistine, anti-intellectual, brutalizing kill-'em-all organizations and postures.

Lyndon Johnson is America, but not all of it, not even a fraction of what is meaningful and lasting in it. Let's not take the way of the powerless and pray — with hate focused on America — for the demise of the U.S.A. Let's hope the Johnsons and Rusks go down — and quickly. But let's not fool around with fantasy where reality is needed: an America which blows up takes Canada with her — not merely because we is small an' dey is big. What's good in America is what we in Canada have most in common with America. If that goes, all goes.

I see the possibility of a president and a cabinet not at all as bleary and rigid and anal as this one Johnson now leads. So don't identify the U.S.A. with a government or Americans with their temporary leaders.

A country which elected, but survived, McKinley, Harding, Coolidge, Hoover, and Nixon as vice-president can't be all bad.

The Parable of the Seventh Seal

Lionel Kearns

This story is about the Seventh Seal, who wasn't really a Seal at all but an imaginative young Polar Bear who wanted to become one.

You see, there was once a small community of impoverished Eskimos who for years had been preyed upon by a pack of stealthy and seemingly invincible Wolves. The Eskimos worked hard all year carving beautiful fat little figures in stone and printing out a few Christmas cards. But every year, just as the Eskimos were getting ready for their Thanksgiving Festival and looking forward to their slack season when they would be able to sit back and rest and dance and make love in peace under the comfort of their warm blankets or in the intimacy of their kayaks, it would happen.

Bam, bam, bam, the Wolves would be roaring into town in their sporty new Ski-Doo snow scooters and their big powerful Bombardier snowmobiles to gather up the whole year's produce, while the Eskimos would stand around shivering with fright in anticipation of another winter without adequate clothing or food or oil to burn in their lamps to brighten the midday gloom of their igloos. The Wolves would stalk around for a few days shooting up the restaurants and ravishing Eskimo girls in the snow banks whenever they could get their paws on them. It was also the Wolves' policy to force the whole population to eat shit.

"Damn good for ya, Boy," they would say. "Nothing like a mouthful of wolf-turd to make an Eskimo realize what's what."

Though this kind of behaviour may seem like mere perversity, it was in fact an important and integral part of the Wolves' over-all program, for according to the political ideology to which they subscribed, trade must follow conquest. If they were to take in the wealth of the Eskimo villagers without forcing something of their own on their victims, the whole Wolf economy would collapse because of the inflationary pressure brought on by an unfavourable balance of payments. So it was that the Wolves exported vast quantities of shit, creating a demand for it by TV advertising, phoney sweepstakes, and outright force of arms.

This was the pattern year after year, with the Eskimos becoming more and more broken in spirit and health. Some even felt they were lucky to be left alive at all, and these were the ones who would go out to welcome the Wolves and fawn on them, hoping to win some small favour such as the right of exclusive local distribution of a new flavour of Wolf shit that had recently been developed. But there were others among the Eskimos who had different ideas.

"Better to die than eat shit," they whispered to one another. "Let's fight."

The Eskimos, however, had no experience or knowledge of conflict, and for this reason they determined to enlist the support of some Seals, who in those days were traditionally bred and trained in the skills of maintaining human dignity.

"Do you ever think the proud Seals will humble themselves by defending us, poor Eskimos that we are?"

"I think so, as long as we do not degrade ourselves by eating shit in their presence."

And so the Eskimos sent off a secret delegation to try to persuade the Seals to help them, and as it turned out they were able to find six willing Seals and one Polar Bear who wanted to be one, and who, because it was an emergency, was called the Seventh Seal. At first the other Seals resented the presence of this alien among their ranks because of his unorthodox proposals, such as shooting flowers at the Wolves instead of bullets. However, eventually they grew to love and respect him, for it was he who was ultimately to play the most significant role in the struggle, as you will learn in a moment.

To begin with, the Seals organized the Eskimos and taught

them self-respect and how to defend themselves and how to see through the semantic traps of the Wolf shit advertisements. When the Wolves discovered what was going on, they zoomed in with napalm and poison gas and lazy-dog, fragmenting anti-personnel bombs which killed large numbers of Eskimos, especially women and children.

But the Wolves couldn't beat the Eskimos, and the Eskimos couldn't beat the Wolves. From the Eskimos' point of view, fighting to the death was better than eating shit, and from the Wolves' point of view, exporting death was as economically sound as exporting shit.

So the struggle went on and on, with no real solution in sight until the Seventh Seal, being a Polar Bear, was able to infiltrate the enemy lines and move around a bit back in Wolfland where he found out to his surprise that some of the Wolves, especially the younger ones, weren't really as inhuman as he had once believed. Their problem, as he saw it, stemmed from the fact that they were all hooked on their own product. The shit they were consuming themselves was poisoning their souls. Break their habit, he thought, and he would abolish the monstrous specter of Wolfhood.

And so it was that while the massive Wolf armies with all their technological superiority were battering the Eskimo villages and trying to contend with the roving bands of Seal-led Eskimo guerillas who would tunnel through the snow and attack the Wolves in the flank, the Seventh Seal, who was really a Polar Bear, was hoofing it around Wolfland showing the Wolf-kids how to turn on with Poetry.

"You just take a poem, roll it into a joint, and smoke it."

And they did, and they liked it, and they told their friends, and before long a whole generation of young Wolves, despite police harassment and the reactionary pressure of commercially controlled mass media, was turning away from the shitty habits of their parents. It was a revolution. Without their daily doses of shit, the Wolves stopped growling and snarling at each other, and as soon as this happened they started to get interested in things like love and creation.

"Come on, Mom, stop eating that stuff and come here and sit down with me and have a small smoke on this poem."

Instead of eating their shit they began burying it, and

some of them actually started to indulge in such unheard of activities as carving stone and making Christmas cards of their own. Gradually they began to realize that there was no reason at all for the war, and so they gave it up. The Eskimos rejoiced in their victory and went back to their simple and productive life.

And so it came to pass that with peace and food and poems distributed *over* the land and all the shit safely *under* it, the Wolves and the Seals and the Polar Bear who was the Seventh Seal and the Eskimos all settled down to love one another and rejoice in the warmth and dignity of their own humanity.

The Preacher and
The President

Edward McCourt

On an autumn Sunday morning in the year 1967, the President of the United States attended divine service in Williamsburg, Virginia. With characteristic humility he sat in what had once been George Washington's favourite pew. From the pulpit the rector, the Reverend Coatsworth Pinckney Lewis, asked a question of the President. "There is a rather general consensus that what we are doing in Vietnam is wrong," he said. "While pledging our loyalty, we humbly ask *why*?"

The fact that the preacher's question has not yet been answered — and may never be — is unimportant. What is important is that the question was asked.

No other nation under heaven has ever fallen so completely victim to its own folklore as has the United States. In other English-speaking lands, the exploits of Robin Hood and his Merry Men inspire youngsters up to the age of twelve to arm themselves with bows and rubber-tipped arrows and shoot down the bad guy (the Sheriff of Nottingham) who falls always to rise again; a balladeer's recital of the exploits of the Black Douglas — hero of a hundred border brawls — serves merely as a prelude to a communal rendition of "Scots Wha Hae" and the "Road to the Isles" and toasts to the "King Over the Water" drunk in amity by both Scot and Sassenach; and even in Ireland tales of the Wild Geese and Robert Emmet and Wolf Tone — all that delirium of the brave — no longer incite the natives to plant bombs in English mailboxes.

The American folk heritage is something else again. Its influence extends through not merely childhood but all of life; the ideals it transmits are lethal and the weapons real.

American folk heroes are almost without exception gunmen — from the wilderness scouts and mountain men who killed, or were killed by, the Indians without pity to the quick-on-the-draw frontiersmen of the old West — Davy Crockett, Wild Bill Hickok, Bat Masterson, Wyatt Earp, Billy the Kid, the James boys, the Dalton boys, and a hundred more. Killers all of them, who shot men down for profit, reputation, security, and sometimes just for fun.

They are long since dead, these heroes of the old West. But the code they lived and died by is still with us, cherished by men who live in suburbia and attend PTA meetings, drive Cadillacs and try to talk like John Wayne.

Born of revolution and scarred, perhaps to the end of whatever years remain to her, by one of the bloodiest civil wars in history, the United States has had troubles growing up. Time was, though, when great crises cast up great leaders. But the gun still rules. The greatest leader they shot — and one who might have achieved greatness. (John Wilkes Booth and Lee Harvey Oswald were merely the trigger men for all those who hated and lacked the courage to be damned.) But now the tradition of the great leader in time of the need of greatness has petered out; gunmen rule the Pentagon and a gunman sits in the White House. Under their guidance the young men who, if they survive the jungles of Vietnam, will be the citizenry of the Great Society, are being brutalized by one of the most futile and hideous of all wars ever fought; and at home whites and Negroes buy guns with which to kill one another in an impending local Armageddon.

Why?

The United States is a powerfully muscled, fast-growing, tormented adolescent who has been forced to assume, within the last quarter-century, responsibilities which demand maturity, patience, cunning, forbearance — all the attributes and qualities with which the adolescent is least adequately endowed. But there is an easy way, a way hallowed by folklore and the movies, to resolve all difficulties, to eliminate all threats, real or imagined. A way which has worked from the halls of Montezuma to the shores of Tripoli. (So why not in Vietnam?) Diplomatically inept the United States may be, but she is expert on the draw. The adolescent reaches for his gun the way his heroes did. But the gun he draws is no longer a six-shooter; it is a nuclear warhead, an ICBM, a hydrogen bomb.

This is why the preacher's question is important. Not the question itself but the fact of its being asked. So long as an ordinary citizen can ask a question of his president, so long as there is hope that enough citizens will ask enough questions, there is hope that the United States, given time enough, will in fact provide the kind of enlightened world leadership which, by virtue of her strength and her wealth and her genius she is — in all things except wisdom — already so admirably fitted to provide.

Her doom — and with it that of all the nations of earth — is not inevitable until no one asks a question of the president.

Lyndon Johnson and Bismarck's Ghost

Alden Nowlan

What the United States government needs more than anything else is a healthy dose of honest cynicism. The most frightening thing about Lyndon Johnson is that he obviously believes his own speeches. Johnson, in fact, is the most dangerous kind of politician: an idealist.

He could be forgiven for calling South Vietnam a bastion of freedom if he were only placating the electorate or soothing the consciences of his country's allies and satellites. And he can hardly avoid pretending that the American forces in Vietnam are defending a small but gallant democracy against a powerful and ruthless aggressor, even when this pretense compels him and his government to invent a "Republic of Vietnam" as purely imaginary as Zenda or Graustark. In this era of mass-produced ideology, all heads of state are required to talk that kind of nonsense. What's terrifying is that Johnson thinks he's telling the truth.

This tough Texan has fought and schemed his way from a country schoolhouse to the White House. Where practical politics are concerned, he could give lessons to Machiavelli. Yet so powerful is the American Dream, so all-pervasive is American idealism, that he has somehow managed to retain the awful innocence of a high school valedictorian or a Woodrow Wilson.

And, God help us, Goldwater was even more of an innocent, a fugitive from Little Orphan Annie. Rockefeller and Romney have yet to qualify for their tenderfoot scout badges. And, in the background, astride a white horse, sixguns strapped low on his hips, looms the greatest and most dangerous innocent of them all, Wild Ron Reagan, sheriff of Tombstone, successor to Kit Carson and Babe Ruth.

What's needed is a Bismarck — or, at the very least, a Grover Cleveland or a Louis Philippe, a man who can distinguish between what is real and what is imaginary and who knows words are not things but symbols.

The United States is doomed to be an empire.

The day the western frontier reached the Pacific Ocean it was inevitable that the United States would become a power in Asia. For more than a century, the United States has been extending and strengthening its Asiatic empire. Under Chiang Kai-shek, China was as much an American possession as India was a British. George III went mad when he lost his thirteen American colonies; the United States went a little mad when it lost China.

This is not a moral judgment, although it will be taken as such because, for complex historical and ideological reasons, both of today's great empires, the American and the Russian, indignantly deny that they are imperialistic.

Actually, if moral standards can be applied to the effects of geographical and economic necessity, it can be argued convincingly that American imperialism is the most benevolent in history. It is quite possible that Vietnam would be better off, in most respects, as a colony or protectorate of the United States than as an independent country. Certainly, our own politicians and economists assure us that Canada, as an economic satellite and military protectorate of the United States, is wealthier than it could hope to be as a sovereign state.

The trouble is that since the United States has never admitted that its empire exists, the president, who is emperor of half the world, must act as if he were still the head of a little agrarian republic along the Atlantic seaboard. Lyndon Johnson carries this attitude to the extreme when he speaks as though the thirteen colonies, having expelled the Redcoats and the Hessians, were now defending themselves against an invasion from Vietnam. He seems to suggest that the day after the Americans withdraw from Saigon, Mao Tse-tung will lead an army into Washington.

Worst of all, this isn't just the way he talks. It is the way he thinks. That's what makes him so dangerous.

Consider what such a man might learn from old Bismarck, who knew what empires were all about. Imagine the two of them, the Primitive Baptist idealist and the noble Prussian cynic, sitting down together in the White House.

Bismarck: Mr. President, the economists and the general staff have explained most carefully the advantages of our annexing Indochina to our empire. Economically —

Johnson: Pardon me, Prince, but let's get one thing straight, right from the beginning. The United States is only interested in maintaining the territorial integrity and national sovereignty of our good neighbours in Southeast Asia. As I've said many times before —

Bismarck: I stand corrected, Mr. President. Now, if I may continue. The economists and the general staff have explained in painstaking, almost painful detail why it is important that we, ah, maintain the territorial integrity of our Indochinese protectorates —

Johnson: No, no, no, Prince. Not protectorates, the free people of the great Republic of South Vietnam. We must honour our commitments to the distinguished Prime Minister — er, his name slips my mind right at the moment, but we can look it up later. Whenever there's a new one they run his picture on the cover of *Time*. Big Minh, I think the fellow's name is. Or Little Minh or something. Anyway, he's a great friend of the free world, and this great nation is pledged —

Bismarck: To be sure, to be sure, Mr. President. But to speed up our discussions might it not be better if we spoke English and had our decisions translated later by the state department or one of *Life*'s editorial writers?

Johnson: Prince, that's exactly what we want: a frank exchange of viewpoints at the summit level, a —

Bismarck: Quite. Now, Mr. President, I have prepared some estimates similar to those which I used in the matters of Schleswig-Holstein and Alsace-Lorraine — both highly profitable real estate operations undone by my idiotic successors. I would estimate, first of all, that Vietnam is worth a maximum of $5,000,000 per square mile per month. No more. I would further estimate that we might well afford to spend 250 dead per month. Under certain circumstances, I would be willing to spend 300 dead, but that would be the absolute maximum. Note that the $5,000,000 I quoted includes the cost of napalm, phosphorous, bribing native politicians, hiring mercenary troops, etc. Later, we can consider each item separately, if you like.

Johnson: Hold on a minute, Prince. We're talking about this as though it were a business deal. I want you to know America is involved in a holy crusade against the forces of godless communism. We're —

Bismarck: Please, Mr. President, wait until I've finished. If you examine the figures, you will see that Vietnam is already costing us more than $5,000,000 per square mile per month and is likely to cost still more. Furthermore, we are spending more dead than we can well afford. Logic suggests that we cut our losses and invest elsewhere — perhaps in Cambodia or Thailand or even in Aden. Personally, I lean towards Thailand, which is still a reasonably cheap commodity. I shouldn't wonder if we could get it for less than $2,000,000 per square mile per month and, oh, perhaps, twenty-five dead per month for the next twenty-five or thirty years — a trifling price to pay, just enough, really, to inspire the proper patriotic fervour . . . .

Johnson: But, Prince, you're talking as though these matters were decided by common sense. We don't use common sense in deciding the foreign policy of the United States.

Bismarck: Alas, Mr. President, what you have said is only too true. I believe, on second thought, that I will return to the relative calmness and sanity of Valhalla.

New Jersey: 1935

Dorothy Livesay

In the landlady's garden
we walked entwined in moonlight
Luella and I
tree and shadow of tree
linked white and black.
It was a time
before this present darkness
before flashes of violence
tore clouds with lightning crack —
but in the moonlight
we were visible
walking the landlady's garden
we were seen entering her house
climbing upstairs for supper.
And when Luella had left
(at least she waited till I closed the door)
the landlady shoved her shoulder
into mine
        and her frog eyes
into my face:
"Was that a coloured girl you dared to bring
into my home?"
"Why, yes, a social worker;
we have jobs together in the Settlement House."
"For that I could whack
the liver out of anyone. Don't ever
let a nigger enter my door again."
"Why no! — I never will —

nor a white girl, either."
And I went upstairs
to pack.

> They say it's the same thing, now
> even in the North, the same
> animal fear, frog eyes —
> and in response
> the same dark guttural laugh:
> "You jest don' understand things, honey."
>
> And I guess I don't understand
> for I haven't been back.

The Generation of Hunters

Dave Godfrey

Southern California flashes constant warnings to you about your body stenches and ignores its own. In a bar in San Diego, on your way to be interviewed for a job you don't really want, there is always this Marine: heavy-fleshed, loquacious, his uniform immaculate, still on top of his liquor, nameless as all Bobs and Jimmies are nameless.

He's been around. He doesn't mind that you're drinking Canadian Club — he likes the ads — but he'll stay on beer. Sure, he knows Kenora and the Whiteshell, anybody from Duluth way does. Man, he'd like to get back there; but he's been on a bad detail, for a year, escort for the dead. But it gets him around. Fresh back from Tennessee yesterday. On detail. A punk. Just a punk. Wrapped his Chevy around a pole on the way to Mexico. After whores. But his body returns home with an escort. *Now* they're getting some real heroes though, that's one thing you can say for Vietnam. He doesn't have a lot to say for Vietnam; unlike many he avoids the regular terms of hate. When his memory of change within his life comes out, it's a neat well-packaged story, an accepted memento; like a St. Christoper medal wound about with Saran-wrap against a time of fear, or simply protected against the grit that enters the cleanest of pockets. He speaks his story without a slur, with mere traces of a rapid-fire stuttering.

We had always been bothered by bears while berry picking. That year my father left with the 303 and just four shells. "Don't waste anything you don't have to," he said. "You're in a war."

That war had been going on for what seemed forever to

me. As soon as it was over I was going to get to practice real shooting again, instead of just sighting and squeezing. As soon as it was over, I told myself, a lot of things would change. It was 1943; I was fifteen years old.

"Take care of yourselves," my father said.

Ginny cried some. The other girls were older.

"Don't tire yourself out on the drill floor," my mother said to him.

Which wasn't what she meant. In late summers like this, when the blueberries came ripe, we would go to my father's hunting shack for what my mother called a shit-and-haddock vacation. "Shit-and-haddock vacations," she would say, "are what you get when you marry a drill sergeant instead of a pilot lieutenant."

Aunt Virginia had married a bush pilot from Duluth who was now overseas and sending back more money than enough. She got around all the bars in Duluth and told tales to my mother. "What he's drilling during the day," she would say, "may be wearing pants; but let me tell you, honey, at night the drilling ain't through khaki. Cotton, or maybe silk. Midnight black or sin-time red. Better believe it, honey."

Out on the blueberry hills at least we kept to our own schedule. We escaped the driving rages my father brought home from the drill hall. We escaped the bitterness my mother mortared back at him. Early in the morning we found a rich area and picked until noon. Then we went back to the shack for lunch and sorted the berries into two grades. In the afternoon we would sometimes go out again for more. Or swim in the river.

With the 303 in my hands, I didn't feel like a picker. I was the sentry, and there were Germans everywhere. Always four of them. I would get the first three quick, always in a vital. Instantaneous death. Heart or head for hellshots; legs for the lazy; stomachs for sadists. I didn't even know what a sadist was. I was a hellshot.

Except if I didn't pick, my mother drove Ginny and the other girls something terrible. It was her only way of getting to me.

"Come on, general," she would say. "We need one man, at least."

I would lay the 303 nearby and pick, with my eyes roving through the woods like a searchlight. Or so I thought. We weren't bothered until the Saturday of the third week. My father was due Sunday morning. The two cubs and the old lady had got halfway to the big bush we were working on before I saw them. It was almost like I had planned. I moved off from the bush to keep my line clear. My stomach was on the moss; my elbows on flat granite. I remembered everything my father had showed me those years before the war, when he knew the war was coming and didn't know how long it would last and wanted me to be a hellshot before the shells got too rationed.

I hit the first cub clean, and while the old lady bent over him, I hit the second one clean. And she roared at that, a sound like a dog trying to say "ground." She came towards the sound of the gun, stood up on her back legs to see where I was. So I got her in the stomach. It wasn't where I'd wanted to, but it was where I'd hit her. I could almost see her pain. Like the first time I'd had beer. She went back to the cubs and then she went back to the woods. Loping like a man hid in a gorilla suit.

I *knew* she wouldn't go far, which was my mistake. Because I could have got her in the head, through the back of the brain, easy enough. But I wanted to have that fourth shell still there when my father got back, and instead it was a week and a day before we found that old lady. Alone, I lost her even before it got dark.

All that next Sunday my father made me walk with him, and I didn't say a word, so that I felt like I lived in a house with a stopped-up toilet. Which was what he wanted. All that week I didn't pick because I was sure I could find her, but I couldn't.

And the next Sunday, when we did find her, I found out what my father meant about gut-shots, about stomachs for the sadists. She was in a little swampy hollow. "Any animal goes low to die," my father said. And she was covered with swarms of black flies, so that trying to see her was like trying to get to your bed in a strange room. My father took out the skull and cleaned it. The stench made me want to be sick, but

I knew what he would say. I got the gun ready. For then he did what I knew he would do. He set the skull up at a hundred yards and made me put the shell I'd thought I'd saved into it, into the shattering bone and brain matter.

"Sometimes you have to waste something," he said.

When the war was over, my father left for Oregon. "Your mother can look after the girls," he told me. "You'll be okay on your own." I knew I would be.

When Aunt Virginia's husband came home from the war, he was an alcoholic, and he died slowly under government care in a VA hospital. The government took care of our needs too, because my father had been a soldier in both wars, even if just a drill sergeant in the second one. I signed up myself in forty-nine. Been in ever since. I guess you must have done your bit a little later?

A bove the bar where we drink, the big Coors ad of fireworks bursting across a four-by-three square of plastic night continues its cycle in many colours. If you have the patience, or the desire, you can figure out the cycle. This next one will be red, you can say, of the imitation of Roman candle that arches its way into nothingness. Yellow. Blue. Green. Yin. Red. Blue. Yang. The sun which pales. There are times when you seem conscious of observing inevitability.

Winning

George Bowering

The priests are blessing guns again,
sending men to their knees
before their graves.

In time of kings
the golden throne
grew higher with each dead soldier.

Now dead soldiers
buy new Cadillacs with bucket seats
for citizens
who own
factories.

> Our sons are dying in Asia
> cries the senator
> who signed the paper
> to make the bombs
> to drop on the smile of Asia

> "Peace," whispers the sergeant squeezing the trigger.
> "Peace," shouts the president signing the paper.
> "Peace," say the voters, empty-eyed
>   on their lawns of Asian skin.
> "Peace," is the sound of jelly gas
>   taking the living pants off a hillside,
>   skin off a girl's back.

& the bleeding muscles cry "Peace."

Peace be with you say the priests in Asia,
& they wear U.S. Army boots,
the rubber soles notched for war.

The general says Peace
is Victory, whose dream of Victory
is blood oozing from the brain.

Victory is to the God of War his praise
who never sought for Peace,
who twists a man in his fire
& stamps an eagle on him,

prey-bird that falls on pigeons
like jet fighters
on the lonely bicycles of Asia.

   "Peace" — the sergeant holds his machine gun.
   "Peace" — the priest holds his silver cross.

   The Eagle laughs.
   He is 50,000 feet above the ground
   of Asia.

Boil Me No Melting Pots, Dream Me No Dreams

Larry Zolf

When the Fathers of Confederation built this country in 1867, there was universal agreement among *all* Canadians, English- and French-speaking, that there was no place for the American Dream on the northern half of this continent. In 1776 we embraced the United Empire Loyalists and rejected George Washington's Revolutionary Army by force of arms. We booted Uncle Sam in the pants in 1812 and slapped his wrists in the Fenian Raids of the 1880's. We rejected slavery and provided sanctuary for American Negroes fleeing that "peculiar institution."

We rejected republicanism, the American idea that the people in and of themselves can shape their own ends and destinies. We countered Jacksonian democracy with the responsible government of a constitutional monarchy and made it plain to our southern neighbours that there were higher forces shaping our destinies than the untutored rabble of the untouched West. And while we did agree with the Yankee that life and liberty were inseparable, we differed in our pursuit of happiness. In Canada, that pursuit didn't necessarily entail égalité and fraternité. We flatly rejected the American egalitarianism of the Western frontier and the American fraternity of the melting pot.

Canada was conservative country, the land of particularity. The entity known as Anglo-Saxon British Canada was prepared to tolerate the particularity of French Canada and the Slavic-German-Jewish-Oriental particularities of the Golden West, provided all accepted the British monarchy, the British connection, the British rules of the British game as the summum bonum underlying all these particularities.

This, then, was the lay of this land in the year 1926 when an obscure ex-Tzarist draft-dodger and ex-infantryman in Alexander Kerensky's Revolutionary Army decided to emigrate to these shores. That dashing, mustachioed, bulbous-nosed Polack of the Judaic persuasion was none other than Yoshua Falk Zholf, son of Reb Yisroael Zholf, husband to Freda Rachel Zholf, father to Meyer, Reisel, and Judith Zholf, and father-to-be to son-to-be yours truly.

My father was a dreamer. In his youth he dreamed of a Russia where life and liberty were inseparable, where a Jew could freely pursue happiness. In 1914 he was a draft-dodger, moving from city to city and village to village.

When the Tzar was toppled in February, 1917 and Alexander Kerensky proclaimed liberty and equality, my father came out of hiding, drafted his own personal revolutionary manifesto, and presented it to a recruiting officer in Kerensky's army. It read:

> To the Russian Revolutionary Army:
> Dear Sirs: Whereas, I, Falek Zholf, have hitherto refused to shed my blood for the bloody Tzar Nikolai the Second, enemy of my people, and, whereas, the great Revolution has freed my people, and all other peoples that inhabit Mother Russia, I today present myself in payment of my holy debt of loyalty to my fatherland.

My father's revolutionary dreams of brotherhood quickly came to naught. He was sickened by Kerensky's execution of soldiers with Bolshevik sympathies, sickened by Bolshevik execution of nationalists, and soon he and his family were threatened by the vicious anti-Semitism of the Polish government of Pilsudski and Sikorski.

Still my father continued to dream. There was the pastoral dream of life on the land in communion with the sky and the stars and all that, but the Polish government took his land away. There was the dream of pioneering in Palestine, but the Zionists wanted only single men. There was the dream of America, the new homeland of his three brothers, but the goddess Liberty had shut her eyes and gates to Europe's teeming, huddled masses.

Suddenly along came Canada, the British colony that dreamed no dreams and offered Pa, the peasant, a chance to join the Gallician garlic-eaters that were cultivating the flat-lands of the Canadian Golden West.

All this is by way of introduction to a fundamental con-fusion in my father's life which led to a subsequent funda-mental confusion in my life. My father ultimately drifted into Winnipeg and renewed an occupation he once pursued secret-ly in Poland at some risk to his own life — the teaching of Jewish liberal-socialist values to Jewish children. He became first a teacher and then the principal of the Isaac Loeb Peretz Folk School in Winnipeg. This school was a branch of a school system and school curriculum with central headquart-ers in New York City.

Herein lay the rub. My father, unaware of all the trouble Sir John A. and the Fathers had gone to, just naturally as-sumed that Canada was part of the American Dream. His admission to this country he regarded as a miracle. He looked on Canada as a place where Americans sent people they didn't really want to have *now* but might take in later on, provided that while here they were always on good behaviour. In a sense, he regarded Canada as America's Australia — a tem-porary penal colony for temporary undesirables.

As my father's English was not very good and his reading material was strictly confined to Yiddish books and news-papers that came from New York, it was not surprising that Pop soon came to regard Winnipeg as just another borough of Gotham-on-the-Hudson.

The more he read his New York Yiddish newspapers the more he got excited by the American Dream! Who could blame him? The New York paper told of Jewish wonders that poor old Pop could scarcely have imagined in the dreary Polish village that was once his home. Not only could Jews own land in the U.S.A., but, miracle of miracles, wonder of wonders, Jews were actually trusted in America. In the Soviet Union they were purging Trotsky, Kamenev, and Zenoviev. In America they were electing Herbert Lehman governor of New York State. Didn't Roosevelt have a Morgenthau in his cabinet? Weren't Felix Frankfurter, Sam Rosenman, and Ben Cohen FDR's bosom buddies? America was indeed the land of milk and honey; its streets were paved with Jews.

It was natural, almost proper, that my father should have

passed the American Dream on to me, his youngest and the first to be born on the very soil of Canada-America. Until I was thirteen years old, I was enrolled in the day school section of the Isaac Loeb Peretz Folk School. My father was my teacher. There I learned to read from a Yiddish Dick and Jane, Max and Molly primer. It was in Yiddish that I first read *Huckleberry Finn, Tom Sawyer,* and *Moby Dick.* For extra grabbers my father threw in a Jewish *Children's History of the Life and Times of Eugene V. Debs, The Life and Times of Samuel Gompers,* and *The Life and Times of Emma Goldman.* At the tender age of nine, I knew that Franklin D. Roosevelt was God the Father, David Dubinsky of the International Ladies Garment Workers Union was God the Son, and Sidney Hillman of the Amalgamated Clothing Workers of America was God the Holy Ghost.

At the tender age of twelve, I won my first essay contest. The subject was Statue of Liberty poetess, Emma Lazarus, as described by the then Wunderkind of Winnipeg, borough of Manhattan, in these immortal words: "Emma Lazarus was not only a daughter of Israel but a daughter of the world." The next year I capped my success with a bar mitzvah speech triumph that extolled the virtues of Meyer Levin, bombardier on Captain Colin Kelly's *Spirit of America* and the only Jew decorated for bravery at Pearl Harbor. Knowing a good thing when I saw it, I spoke these immortal words: "Meyer Levin was not only a son of Israel; he was a son of America."

And so was I. As I listened in my teens to my father telling horror stories of gas ovens and lamp shades and watched his heart slowly breaking as the news drifted in of the death of his entire family overseas, it was nice, almost comforting, to cast my eyes south of the border. There I could thrill to the athletic exploits of Barney Ross and Hank Greenberg. I could drool at the succulent beauty of Bess Myerson, Miss America, 1946. I could cry tomorrow with Lillian Roth and call my house a home with Polly Adler.

I can remember staying up all night with the old man, crying and cheering as Harry Truman, who gave us Israel, was given four more years. In high school I defended America in the Korean War and argued that the West Germans were good and the East Germans bad. In college, NATO was groovy, the Marshall Plan divine, McCarthyism a minor aberration.

Today, as I reflect on the validity of my American Dream then and now, a certain sense of nostalgic silliness seems to overtake me. I can understand the validity of the American Dream for my father. In the bitter anti-Semitism of Tzarist Russia and Sikorski's Poland, he was considered sub-human. In Auschwitz and Dachau, he and his fellow Jews were not human at all. In the American melting pot, he was not only human; he was an involved participant, an equal.

As my father saw the American Dream, to be Jewish and human was to be American. Today as I see the American Dream operating in black America and yellow Vietnam, I am forced to conclude that somehow to be *really* human is to be neither Jewish nor American. Today the Jewish community in America is indeed a participant and more than an equal in the power elite of white America. The Jews are close to the top in education, affluence, status. But to black America the Jew is as much whitey as anyone else. The lessons of persecution and humiliation that the Jew picked up on his way to affluence and success he is not prepared to pass on to the Negro way, way below. The American Jew lives in a white neighbourhood, worships in a white, cavernous temple, eats white kosher Chinese food at white Chinese restaurants, has white directors for his white bar mitzvah movies. He likes it that way and is sure *everyone* will understand.

Having richly benefited from the American Dream, he is eager to pass the message, not the benefits, to those less fortunate people abroad. The patriotism of today's American Jewry is awesomely wholesome. American-style democracy has been good for the teeming, huddled Jewish masses. How can it help but be good for the teeming, huddled masses of Vietnam? Our Hebrew boy, Walt Whitman Rostow, is today's Emma Lazarus, offering Lyndon Johnson in true Statue of Liberty style as sanctuary to the misguided peasants of Southeast Asia. Our Hebrew boy, Dr. Edward Teller, Pop to the H-bomb, is today's real-life Dr. Sivana, just itching to say "Shazam" and watch the world disappear.

I must admit that my stomach feels queasy when I hear Nicholas Katzenbach and Dean Rusk gloating over the Viet

Cong kill toll, the damned dead of American-style democracy. And I must admit to a similar type of queasiness when I hear Jews gloating over Arab losses in the Six-Day War, the damned dead of Zionist-style democracy, even though I know you shouldn't compare the two and that Nasser will fry me whenever he gets the chance. I also feel queasy whenever I hear bigots, Birchers, and Lubor Zinks praising to the skies the Jewish victory over "Arab communism."

It saddens me to see how the American Dream and the melting pot have coarsened and vulgarized my racial con-frères. The gentleness of East European Jewish Hassidism, the sweet music of the soft, humane Yiddish culture is no longer there. I guess I prefer the schlemiel wisdom of Gimpel the Fool to the Sammy Glick-shtick of Norman Podhoretz. I'd rather walk the crooked, narrow streets of Chagall's shtetl than drive through Forest Hills or Shaker Heights.

That brings me to the lay of this land in 1968. Canada has not yet bought the American Dream. It's still conservative country, the land of particularity. I know the Hebrew particularity ain't quite as yet the equal of other particularities. I know that living here is still a trip backwards in the time tunnel.

Still, I'm glad to be here and to be a Canadian, whatever that word means. I'd rather be somewhat of an outsider in Canada than an equal, accepted participant in the American nightmare.

I am aware that we have avoided American pitfalls more by accident than by design. I realize that we don't have America's responsibilities and therefore her problems. Well, huzzah, I'm glad we don't and to hell with the reasons.

Huzzah, we're not in Vietnam. Huzzah, we won't go there. Huzzah, we never will. Huzzah, we have no Watts-Newark-Detroit. Huzzah, we don't intend to build them.

I'm also aware that my country is in a state of disarray and flux. The old order is crumbling, and all institutions are open to criticism and review. I like that. In my own little way, here in Canada I can be a minor revolutionary, albeit a gutless one, a sort of chicken-hearted Trotsky.

I know that my country has not quite made up its mind about what it wants to be. It has ceased being British and, thankfully, has not yet become American. If there is anything still valid to the British heritage left us by the Fathers of Confederation, let it be this:

Let the country continue to be a land of un-American activities. Boil me no melting pots and dream me no dreams. Worry not, rumour has it that God is Dead. If so, he can't bless America.

The What Is To Be Done Poem

Phyllis Webb

The denial of one's neighbour is
easy / as
denial of one's self / the me
-keeping silence.
But to hold the alert passions
pointing around the sun is
what must be done
beloved (oh my!) America / lost
land of the New Found
-ling conscience. Do the sun
flowers over the border still
find their heads to the sun?
What Is To Be Done? the old
sob of Chernyshevsky who /
holding his head to the wall of the
great cell of Russia / how many
years ago / cried out some
kind of answer. But now "to be
done" is what harrows us / here
in our Iceland / here in our me-
keeping silence of no letters no
poems policy right action ever /
and ever the empty prevarications of
"I am sorry for the delay." Who wants
you for a neighbour? You hit
at the hope of whoever believed
Vanzetti and Sacco ("Those beautiful
clove flowers surprised me so deeply

in my unrest heart . . .") once lay / in
the palm of your justice. They learned
the hard way. Died with the grace
of the pure in heart.
But how shall we die who are not /
pure not pure?
And if the burning bush is not the
spirit in-living who's to say
that the saffron robe dancing in flames
is the phoenix arising?

There are too many heroes these days
and a sweet nostalgia for wisdom.
I would not judge in a book of /
judgment. I can kill with a word or
the keeping-me-silence / or
turn my sun flower head to that
Burn Baby Burn!
/ or the now-coming-love of
perhaps or at least a short season
/ or Shanti shanti shanti
as an / old cat said
(Mistah Kurtz — he dead?)
and sun flower seed are
for parrots?

A New Nest of Eagles

Henry Beissel

In a letter dated June 11, 1823, Jefferson, comparing the United States with the "nations of eternal war" in Europe, wrote:

> On our part, never had a people so favourable a chance of trying the opposite system, of peace and fraternity with mankind, and the direction of all our means and faculties to the purpose of improvement instead of destruction.

The chance was missed. Today the United States is by far the most belligerent member of the disunited family of nations. Her economy is more permanently a war economy than that of any other nation in the modern world. Her troops are deployed all over the globe flying the colours of the menacing eagle that Hawthorne describes, "with outspread wings, a shield before her breast, and . . . a bunch of intermingled thunderbolts and barbed arrows in each claw. With the customary infirmity of temper that characterizes this unhappy fowl, she appears, by the fierceness of her beak and eye, and the general truculency of her attitude, to threaten mischief to the inoffensive community." Once the pride of Prussia and Rome, the eagle with her arrogance of nobility and power is emblematic of an attitude and a manner of conduct that are irreconcilable with the egalitarian, fraternal, and peaceful principles of American democracy and that have made the United States the most distrusted, the most resented, and even the most hated of nations today.

Almost fifty years before he wrote the letter I quoted, Jefferson proclaimed that "all men are by nature equally free and independent" (1776), and he spelled out the enjoyment of life, liberty, property, happiness, and safety as their inalienable birthrights. These were the ideals embodied in the Constitution of the United States: they fired the imagination of her citizenry, and their pursuit was to create a garden of Eden and a city of God, one after the other, in the New World. But the dream has turned into a nightmare. Everywhere the idiot grins of she-males and cheesecake, bought, packaged, and sold on Madison Avenue in a desperate attempt to feign and insinuate happiness where fear and emptiness prevail! One third of this wealthiest nation on earth lives in substandard conditions, millions of them in actual poverty. For most of the others, the enjoyment of property means a lifetime of anxiety and economic slavery. For them, the problem is equality — an even more severe problem than poverty in a country where one per cent of the population owns one third of the nation's wealth. Education, political rights, health, justice mean one thing to the rich, another to the poor, and yet another to the Negro. Inequality rules American society. What remains of liberty is manipulated into meaninglessness by a deliberately dishonest system of mass communications media and an army of unscrupulous behavioural scientists, market researchers, PR men, and advertisers — all in the service of the maximization of profits for a few and the corrosion of individual choice and character for the multitude.

Abroad too, liberty is synonymous with acceptance of the American tin-pan alley of life. Dissent is either bought or bludgeoned into silence. All over the world American money and American troops are used to prop up dictatorships and to suppress and eradicate national liberation movements.

How is it that a nation which (just in case my polemical discourse should promote smugness at home) has demonstrated and still demonstrates a finer moral fiber, a greater vitality and courage than we have in Canada should surrender to dehumanization, corruption, and violence? The United States has produced great poets and painters, writers, musicians, scientists, thinkers — the best in the New World: how is it that the worst have come to prevail? Why, after less than 200 years, is the reality of American society such a grotesque perversion, such a ghastly parody of its own ideals?

There is no simple or single answer to any of these questions. It is precisely the simple-minded rationalism of the eighteenth century with its romantic optimism and its shallow utopianism about the nature of man and the world that has contributed substantially to America's present dilemma. We don't live in the best of all possible worlds, and it is simply not true that history is synonymous with progress and enlightenment. It is simply not true that men are good and equal and that enlightenment will, as a matter of course, temper their selfishness and bring about paradise.

Considering the immense natural wealth of America and the circumstances of its settlement, it is not surprising that happiness should have come to mean material success. Nor, considering its pragmatic, utilitarian origins and the rigid moralism of puritanism, is it surprising that the political system should have come to approve and promote commercialism. Enter the goddess Usura whose fairy tale forests are a telltale jungle where the fittest that survive are the most cunning and unscrupulous. She rules men by greed and vulgarizes and brutalizes all. *Radix malorum est cupiditas* — America is beginning to taste the bitterness of this. Justice is bought, professional integrity sold; trust is mortgaged, truth auctioned off. Corruption is ubiquitous: in the police force, in government, in labour unions, in the party machinery, in business, in the news media. Bribery, extortion, price-fixing, embezzlement — anything from elementary cheating to murder goes. The new ethic is "crime doesn't pay," which means that everything that pays is not a crime and of course that which is not a crime is ethical. The war in Vietnam pays — millions or perhaps billions to a few, a little bit to everybody. And so even mass murder becomes ethical. In such a climate of dishonesty and violence, crime syndicates can operate openly and profitably. The current wave of riots and increasingly aggressive demonstrations is, ironically, an extension of this violence even though it is a radical protest against the perversion and corruption that produced it. Rapidly the social order of the United States is degenerating into anarchy.

In 1920, the Irish poet Yeats proclaimed the end of Western civilization:

Things fall apart; the center can not hold;
Mere anarchy is loosed upon the world,
The blood-dimmed tide is loosed, and everywhere
The ceremony of innocence is drowned.

Yeats held a cyclical view of history as a series of recurrent patterns of culture. Oswald Spengler, in his brilliant morphological study of history, *The Decline of the West*, examined and described, at the same time as Yeats but independently, the phases of these cyclical patterns and demonstrated the parallel characteristics of many past cultures. In its final phase, he argues, each culture turns into a civilization whose supreme value is always money. Thus the Greek historian Polybius, in the second century B.C., summarized the decline of the Phoenicians by saying, "At Carthage, nothing which results in profits is regarded as disgraceful!" For Spengler, America is such an end-civilization.

Whatever allowance has to be made for the inadequacy of all analogies, the parallels between Rome (the final phase of classical culture) and America (the final phase of European culture) are uncanny. Spengler shows that Rome was cerebral, irreligious, factual, journalistic, analytical, technological, hedonistic, cosmopolitan. So is America. Rome was preoccupied with size and quantity and performed colossal construction feats (roads and buildings). The same is true of America. It was the Emperor Vespasian who championed the American profit ethic when he justified to critics his tax on public urinals: *pecunia non olet* — "money does not smell." Rome was an imperialistic nation; the whole classical world came to fear the beak and claws of the eagles from Capitol Hill. We have a new nest of eagles now on a new Capitol Hill, and the world trembles. Internally corrupt and externally overextended, Rome's empire crumbled, beginning at the faraway perimeters. Is Vietnam the turning point for the U.S.?

Pictures from Vietnam

Michael Ondaatje

The grass ruffles in gasoline wind,
beaches white — are geometry
abstract with oil drums.

The boy with gun
watches her feed a child,
and fingers pluck her breast
and he embarrassed,
lascivious at his mouth.

Beautiful photography
that holds no morality.

Planes came through dawn
threw green red flames
and spilled a paddy field.
Water jumped eleven feet
and fell, and hissed into the fire.
A bullock stood in bones, then dropped.

She laid down child
skull drained of liquid
its side unlaced like tennis shoes

Hooray for the Scars and Gripes!

J. M. S. Careless

The United States is Canada's great cliché. Our reactions to the country and its people have all the hard-worn polish of "it's a nice place to visit" or "some of my best friends." This is inevitably so because Canadians have been worrying over and responding to the United States ever since the American Revolution created both countries by running a political boundary across the mass of North America. Since then we have been obsessed with the far greater magnitude of American power and success: fearing it, resisting it, and leaning on it; criticizing, deploring, and emulating it.

Again this is all but inevitable, since to a very large degree the American presence has shaped Canada. It gave French-Canadians a reason for accepting British imperial rule and then for aligning politically with English-Canadian colonists as the best means to ensure survival in the face of huge American absorptive power. It gave English-Canadians the War of 1812, the one conflict they have fought on their own soil, with its consequent memories of successful national defense to reinforce the original Loyalists' declaration of independence from the United States. And sharp strains during the American Civil War did much to impel the separate British-American colonies to combine in Confederation in 1867 in order to form a political and economic unit big enough to be viable outside of a notably unfriendly republic. In short, through varied impacts with deep historic effect, the United States has served repeatedly, if unwittingly, as the best friend nationalism could have in a country as culturally and sectionally divided as Canada.

The process continued throughout the century after Confederation. American probing into the Northwest, American railroad projects, spurred the building of the C.P.R. The rising wall of the United States tariffs provided sanction for the adoption of Canadian policies of economic nationalism. Then the influx of American capital and techniques, from dry-farming in the West to factory industry in the East, gave increasing breadth and substance to the Canadian continental system. And later improved relations with the United States stimulated a sense of North American defensive security, which had its own consequence in the drive to realize full Canadian nationhood out of the declining British Empire. In striking ways — though certainly not as the only factor — the United States has worked to build the modern Canadian nation.

Obviously, it has no less helped to impair it; for instance, to offer always the seductive charm of giving up: to cease to pay the cost of Canada, either personally through emigration or collectively through annexation by joining the great world of the American union. What country other than Canada exists with the implicit assumption that if we can't go home to Mother anymore, Uncle (supposedly) will always take us in?

Again there is the evident fact that the United States ministers to sectional division in Canada. Pulls to the south ally the various Canadian regions with their more powerful American neighbours, thus thwarting the development of strong east-west ties within Canada herself. Through mass media, as in travel, Canadians look south to New York or Hollywood, to Chicago, Boston, or Miami. And the power of American investment may develop our resources and technology but sap our control and determine our lives within our own country. Everybody has heard about that.

All this indeed is true — but hardly new, dating almost from the time that the two countries first took form. Again it is the inescapable influence of the giant American presence at our side. We have both used and had to pay for superior United States development (superior that is, in terms of time, opulence, and availability) ever since American entrepreneurs opened blast furnaces at Normandale, Ontario in the 1820's or put the steamboat on the Red River in the 1850's. We see the results of American penetration all around us today. Yet what we need also to observe is how this massive and pervasive force has continually invited the reactions which, thus far, have still shaped a separate Canadian entity.

At any rate, it is small wonder that Canadians are thoroughly ambivalent in their response to the United States, another trite adage in our bundle called the great cliché. They must be. Throughout their history they have been so constantly helped or hampered by America and the Americans. But they have always been utterly involved. One is tempted to conclude, in fact, that there could not be a Canada without the United States — and may not be a Canada with one. That uncertainty adds a delicious touch of piquancy to an otherwise bald and unconvincing narrative.

America

John Newlove

Even the dissident ones speak
as members of an Empire, residents
of the center of the earth. Power
extends from their words
to all the continents and their modesty
is liable for millions. How must it be
to be caught in the Empire, to have
everything you do matter? Even
treason is imperial; the scornful
self-abuse comes from outside the boundaries
of the possible. Outside the borders of royalty
the barbarians wait in fear,
finding it hard to know which prince
to believe; trade-goods comfort them,
gadgets of little worth, cars, television,
refrigerators, for which they give iron,
copper, uranium, gold, trees, and water,
worth of all sorts for the things
the citizens of Empire take as their due.

In the Empire power speaks from the poorest
and culture flourishes. Outside the boundaries
the barbarians imitate styles and send their sons,
the talented hirelings, to learn and to stay;
the sons of their sons will be princes too,

AMERICA / *John Newlove*

in the Estate where even the unhappy
carry an aura of world power, and the lords
of power send out their directives
for the rest of the world to obey. If they live
in the Empire, it matters what they say.

Besieged, Neglected, Violated, and Ignored

Naim Kattan

It is never easy to live next door to a giant. Canadians are always conscious of the heavy weight of the American presence in the economy of their country, in its industry, and in research.

It is possible to build abstract structures or to propose a plan of action to attempt to escape from American ascendancy, to advocate a firm policy of economic nationalism and demand that the government take energetic measures to protect the integrity of this country. But such attitudes do not modify, except very superficially, the nature of the relations that each one of us individually, whether he wishes to or not, maintains with the United States — uneasy and ambivalent relations of love and hate, fascination and rejection. We feel at once besieged and neglected, violated and ignored. We resent the Americans' being so intimately involved in our life and at the same time so indifferent to the welfare of our country. Proportionately, we are undoubtedly the nation that consumes the most American products after the United States itself. We take the advantages of the most advanced technology for granted. We avail ourselves of it without having to make the effort of research, development, and discovery ourselves. But we cannot accept with good grace a situation so satisfactory that its loss would be a real privation.

True, we love to go to New York; the stores are more numerous and bigger there, the choice is greater, and above all, the products are familiar to us. We do not seem to be in a foreign country, and no exoticism casts a screen between the city and ourselves. The restaurants are really those of a foreign city — but so similar to our own. We find the same cinemas and, to a certain extent, the same theatres, though in greater number and variety. To us the city offers a model, familiar and colossal, pushing to their utmost limits all the latencies and potentialities of our own. This is our own universe, a world to which we belong, but like all the other Americans, we do not fully accept New York. We maintain, and in this we are quite sincere, that we prefer to be there only in passing, as outsiders.

We also love the American beaches. Of course, we claim that we go there because the water is warmer. This is true. These are beaches whose organization neither dazzles nor shocks us. We find our way about them without effort. How pleasant it is to feel a sense of distance, without paying the full price, to be in a foreign country and yet so much at home. Even exoticism is domesticated here. Foreign sights and dishes of far-off lands will be offered to us, but all have been pre-designed for us.

And then we accept the need to speak English more willingly in New York or Chicago than in Montreal or Ottawa, for there the situation is clear. The U.S. is a foreign country, unilingual and English-speaking. There is no ambiguity. And if we feel wounded at being treated as foreigners in Toronto or Vancouver, even though this is not put in so many words, we expect and even wish to be considered citizens of another country when we are in the United States.

We castigate the U.S. with satisfaction and even joy, we search out Americans' lacks and their faults and take pleasure in dwelling on their weaknesses and the frailty of certain of their institutions. We were among the first to deplore and spurn the Americans' materialism, their pragmatism, their love for the dollar. However, if we examine the real state of affairs, we see that we suffer from the same ills. But to heap one's own shadowy terrors upon others is a common exorcism; our loud cries in the face of American racism make us feel virtuous at small cost to ourselves. We know, though without always admitting it, that if we are not racists it is simply because there are few Negroes among us. We are aware in the depths of ourselves that if American power disturbs us, it also gives us reassurance. There is no boundary more tenuous than that between the desire to be protected and the rejection of the protector.

To some extent we live under privileged conditions with respect to the United States. We can profit from all the advantages of the technical progress of our neighbours while still insisting, whenever we choose, that we do not accept the world their technology is building. But we know, and this distresses us, that our very independence and real autonomy are limited by our wish to nourish ourselves at the sources of this scientific expertise.

I realized some fifteen years ago that it is all too easy to establish one's own identity by a mere opposition to the United States and that to be a Canadian is not simply a matter of not being an American. I asked myself just what it was about America that the Canadian rejected, since in his daily life and certain of his habits he was so American (and I am not speaking just of his sharing the American continent but also of his acceptance of the industrial and technical civilization created by the U.S.). I did not find an answer in the novel or in the poetry of either French or English Canada. I began then to explore contemporary American writing, and this was to me a great revelation, not only of the very particular world that is being built beside us but of ourselves, the present state of this country and its still unsettled future.

The discovery of America is never at an end. All the potentialities that the Americans are beginning now to exhaust are still for Canadians doors opening into hope. We are, far more than are the Americans, still a frontier people. Superficially this makes us seem the little country cousin of the great American metropolitan, younger and not quite so rich as its elder, a little less polished. But we are closer to the innocence the Americans have lost but have not ceased to search for and to a subtlety that comes to us from our mother countries, France and Great Britain, far away but still present because we have not disowned them. We have not known, as have the Americans, an abrupt sundering of the bonds with Europe. The umbilical cord parted slowly, of itself. But if the Canadian is still more attached to the past, this bond is not a line leading him to an identification with the present. And opposition to the United States is simply a means, at little cost, of assuring himself of his own identity.

My reading of the current American writers has enabled me to have a more precise view of Canada. I do not mean to call this a detached view, for everything that threatens Americans — and I have felt it through the agonies and anxieties and questionings of their poets and novelists — weighs upon us too. The United States preceded all other countries in the erection of a post-industrial civilization. We are part of this new era, and we are well aware of this. Perhaps we wish, by our very apparent hostility to the United States, to reject the convulsions and stresses that accompany this new civilization. We may be the first country that will provide the world with an answer to the anxious question that the whole West is putting to itself. Can one safeguard human values; can one avoid the anonymity of the new conformism, while still having full access to the civilization of today? In other words, will Canada be able to keep its own character while availing itself of all the advantages of American life?

It is all too easy to ask the government for political solutions to a problem that is faced by each one of us on a personal level. It is a way of begging the question, of fleeing from reality. We are the first to serve our apprenticeship in the new society that is rising at our side and in our midst. Will we be able to meet the challenge — neither repudiate the new order nor lose ourselves in collective anonymity?

The Decline of America

André Major

Born of a French-speaking Québecois father (a métis by his father and mother) and a mother of Scottish descent, I am French by training and taste, though sensitive also to creative efforts in America. I am, in brief, trying to make myself an original, truly Québecois cultural man by combining several riches. You will realize that this involves me in contradictions, contradictions that on certain days I despair of ever overcoming, though as a writer I must somehow unify the different influences which divide my mind.

Instinctively I distrust the Americans because, though I also live on this continent, I am not bound up in any way with the civilization evolving here. The values of this New World seem to me so old already and so poisoned that I would rather seek refreshment among my own people and in the Old World, where at least the mind has always mastered barbarism, except in moments of grave crisis. This is not the case in North America; here even the most elementary moral sense appears hopelessly warped. It seems to me that, unknown to themselves (for nothing is deliberate with Americans — they act instinctively, and their instinct, as Norman Mailer has noted, is diseased), they are striving to be like the Romans, for whom there was no greater good fortune than to obtain Roman citizenship and live in the Roman style. Americans cannot conceive of any ideal of life but their own, nor can they question that ideal — if we except a few isolated dissidents in the midst of the oblivious crowd. This naivety rests upon a serious misunderstanding: they confuse material power and civilization. They forget that though the Romans pillaged the

Greek heritage, they did so in order to obtain access to Hellenic civilization. But because of their material wealth, the Americans believe they can seduce the whole of humanity, and the whole of humanity does indeed desire a little of this wealth, though without necessarily taking on the burden of the American way of life. India, for example, is dying of starvation, but does she wish to copy America simply in order to be fed? I doubt this. An ancient civilization seldom returns to barbarism. It sinks rather into gentle decadence.

Since I am first and foremost a Québecois — may I be excused for not believing in Canada, a legal fiction bound to splinter under American pressure? — I can see only one solution. To become what history has always intended it to be, Quebec must forge firm and steady bonds with Europe, the uncommitted nations, and South America so that it can resist the pull of the United States. From this viewpoint, the solidarity of the French-speaking countries, the concept of "Frenchness," and de Gaulle's recent visit provide significant guideposts. It remains to be seen whether exchanges between our allies and Quebec will be sufficient to raise a solid barrier between those we like to call the barbarians (in the primary sense of "foreigners") and ourselves, since it must regretfully be admitted that we are a little too Americanized in our habits and our thoughts. The prospect is not utopian if one doesn't believe that the American empire, whose crackings under its own contradictions can be heard already, will endure forever. The grave fault of this military and financial empire is that it offers Americanization when it is a new humanism, founded on respect for other nations, that the world needs. If I may be permitted a rather vague generalization, the Americans achieved power before they had formulated a transcendent vision of the world. In consequence, they are now yielding to fierce and destructive egotism. Blinded by their material power, they are incapable, it is to be feared, of facing up to their own moral failure. They are clearly powerless to solve their social and racial problems at home. But this impotence, far from opening their eyes, does not even prevent their attempting to impose a *Pax Americana* in Vietnam, insupportable as this would be.

True, an intellectual and moral elite is speaking out against the triumphant barbarism of the American people and state, but there is little chance that these voices of reason will be heard. Americans are more responsive to the language of weapons, which they consider more efficient. It is this same efficiency complex that will destroy the United States, will make it pile error upon error, monstrosity upon monstrosity. The best I can hope for is that Americans will die of remorse before the hatred of the world is unleashed against them.

They behave like cruel children with dangerous weapons in their hands, but their innocence doesn't make them less criminal. I wouldn't like to be in their shoes the day they discover the emptiness of their world. I shudder to think that they do not even see the abyss they are digging so lightheartedly between other nations and themselves. But I do not pity these unknowing criminals. No one need pity the strong. Not being a reporter for *l'Express* and having only contempt for the antics of the pro-American French left, I am not in the least fascinated with America. I haven't even considered visiting the country, close to us as it is. My chief feeling towards this monster is indifference. I fear only that its breath will poison the air my people breathe, for I know all too well that their lungs are weak. What irks me is that Europe, except for de Gaulle (the only one who can see beyond parliamentary debates), does not resist the colossus. Europe's exhaustion is the Americans' best ally. Fortunately Asia, Africa, and South America are beginning to raise their heads; these nations are our best hope. If Quebec could free itself from the yoke that is strangling it, I would be happier and would consign the Americans to the devil, praying only that God save the American Negroes. Meanwhile I dream of the day when, disgusted with themselves, the Americans will have the courage to put the torch to their own empire. The human race will not lose very much, and we will be able to look serenely towards the rebuilding of the world.

No, despite the temptation, I will have no share in the artificial paradise of my neighbours. My soul is not for sale. I am still in search of it. So let there be no more distractions.

The Children in Nathan Phillips Square

Dennis Lee

It would be better maybe if we could stop loving the children
and their delicate brawls, pelting across the square in tandem,
      deking
from cover to cover in raucous celebration and they are never
winded, bemusing us with the rites of our own
gone childhood; if only they stopped
mattering, the children, it might be possible, now
while the square lies stunned by noon.
What is real is fitful, and always the beautiful footholds
crumble the moment I set my mind aside, though the world
      does recur.
Better, I think, to avoid the scandal of being — the headlong
particulars, which as they lose their animal purchase
cease to endorse us, though the ignominious hankerings
go on; this induces the ache of things, and the lonesome ego
sets out once again dragging its lethal desires across the world,
which does not regard them. Perhaps we should
bless what doesn't attach us, though I do not know
where we are to find nourishment.
So, in the square, it is a
blessed humdrum: the kids climb over the Archer, and
the pool reflects the sky, and the people passing by,
who doze, and gently from above the visible pollutants de-
      scend,
coating the towers' sheath. Sometimes it
works but once in summer looking up I saw the noxious cloud
      suspended
taut above the city, clenched, as now everywhere it is the

imperial way of life that bestows its fall-out. And it did not
stay inert, but across the fabled horizon of Bay Street they
came riding, the liberators, the deputies of Jesus, the Marines,
and had released bacterial missiles over the Golden Horseshoe
    for love of all mankind,
and I saw my people streaming after calling welcome for the
    small change,
and I ran in my mind crying humiliation upon the country,
as now I do also for it is
hard to stay at the center when you're
losing it one more time, though the pool
reflects the placid sky, and the people passing by, and daily
our acquiescence presses down on us from above and we have
    no room to be.
It is the children's fault as they swarm for we cannot stop
    caring.

In a bad time, people, from an outpost of empire I write
bewildered, though on about living. It is to set down a nation's
failure of nerve; I mean complicity, which is signified by the
gaseous stain above us. For a man who
fries the skin of kids with burning jelly is a
criminal. Even though he loves children he is a criminal. Even
    though his
money pumps your oil he is criminal, and though his
programs infest the air you breathe he is
criminal and though his honest quislings run your
government he is criminal and though you do not love his en-
    emies.
he is criminal and though you lose your job on his say-so he is
    criminal and
though your country will founder without him he is criminal
    and
though he has transformed the categories of your
refusal by the pressure of his media he is a criminal.
And the consenting citizens of a minor and docile colony
are cogs in a useful tool, though in no way
necessary and scarcely
criminal at all and their leaders are
honourable men, as for example Paul Martin.

In Germany, the civic square in many little towns is
hallowed for people. Laid out just so, with
flowers and fountains, and during the war you could come and
relax for an hour, catch a parade or just
get away from the interminable racket of the trains,
clattering through the outskirts with their lousy
    expendable cargo.
Little cafes often, fronting the square. Beer and a chance to
    relax.
And except for the children it's peaceful here
too, under the sun's warm sedation.

The humiliations of imperial necessity
are an old story, though it does not
improve in the telling and no man
believes it of himself.
It is not Mr. Martin who sprays the poison mist
on the fields of the Vietnamese, not in person nor fries
    civilians and if he
defends an indefensible war, making himself a
stooge, making his people accessories to genocide, he is no
worse a man than the other well-intentioned sellouts of his-
    tory —
the Britons who went over to the legionaries, sadly for the
    sake of the larger peace,
the tired professors of Freiburg, Berlin, the statesmen at
    Munich, those
estimable men, and the lovers of peace, the brisk switchers
    who
told it in Budapest. Doesn't the
service of quiet diplomacy require dirty hands?
(Does the sun in summer pour its warm light into the square
for us to ignore? We have our own commitments.)
And then if it doesn't work one is finally
on the winning side though that is
unkind: Mr. Martin is an honourable man, as we are all
Canadians and honourable men.

And this is void, to participate in an
abomination larger than yourself. It is to fashion

other men's napalm and know it, to be a
Canadian safe in the square and watch the children dance and
dance and smell the lissome burning
bodies to be born in
old necessity to breathe polluted air and
come of age in Canada with lies and vertical on earth no man
    has drawn a
breath that was not lethal to some brother it is
yank and chink and hogtown linked in
guilty genesis it is the sorry mortal
sellout burning kids by proxy acquiescent
still though still denying it is merely to be human.

'mericans

Barry Lord

When my three-year-old came home from the Moscow Circus the other night, I expected him to tell me about bears, clowns, and acrobats. Instead, he claimed to have seen the 'mericans. And went to bed talking about the 'merican soldiers he'd watched at the circus. Since I didn't think the cultural exchange program had gone that far, I asked him to explain.

And with a little help from his mother, he described how a Moscow magician had ended his act in a sudden burst of fire and puff of smoke. The flame had reminded the boy of the 'merican soldiers he'd seen on TV, putting the torch to Vietnamese peasants' huts.

I don't remember what my image of the U.S. was when I was three, but I don't believe it was that accurate. We have all been learning a lot in the past few years, so that today even a three-year-old knows that the United States is the agent of destructive fire.

We happen to live next door to the arsonist: I would like to draw the simple conclusion that we must join the volunteer firemen. Let me be specific and ideological. The United States of America today is the last bastion of an economic and political system which was always vicious and exploitative but which is now outmoded as well, so that it profits only its relatively few controllers while bringing misery, famine, and death to most of the rest of the world. In defense of this system, the United States will use any means — *Newsweek* to napalm, subsidiaries to CIA.

The system is called free enterprise, and it was a good idea for a long time. It created the Industrial Revolution, and in the

United States it made a great nation. But beginning a little over a century ago, we began to discover a better way of getting things done, by organizing and working together without the profit margin. They know about it now in places like China, Cuba, Vietnam. China is feeding itself, India is not; Cuba is literate, Guatemala is not; Hanoi is a purposive community, Saigon is a whorehouse. The new system is a better system for more people.

It is important to recognize that the U.S. empire is a regime of violence, not only for black Americans or Vietnamese but in every aspect of life and death. It is free enterprise that causes the horrendous infant mortality rate in every Latin American country except Cuba, that starves the people of India and offers them contraceptives as a solution, that supports the apartheid businessmen of South Africa and the Portuguese murderers in Angola. And it is free enterprise that makes our educational system pointlessly competitive, that packages women as commodities, that drives our young people and artists out to the margins of our community. Think of the daily deaths from hunger and malnutrition alone and know that they could be prevented — and have been prevented in nations outside the U.S. empire. Contrast the barren lives of those supposedly enjoying the fruits of this "free world" with the constructive consciousness of the Red Guard, the cane-cutting Cubans, or the "All Land to the Peasants" Viet Cong. The U.S. empire rules by force and causes death and destruction wherever it holds power; it is the military, economic, social, and psychological source of aggression in the world today.

I am sorry if these remarks sound platitudinous, dogmatic, or dated. But perhaps we have listened long enough to more contemporary sophisticated explanations for the mess we are in. What is the relevance of Marshall McLuhan, Buckminster Fuller, or Timothy Leary to a Bolivian tin miner who knows his child would not be starving if only the vast riches of his country were not controlled by the U.S. empire and the few wealthy Bolivians who govern for it? For that matter, what is their relevance to burning Detroit? Their voices may be heard again after the fall of the empire, when we will have our technology, electronic and chemical, in our own hands. Meanwhile, they serve only to veil the harsh realities of power and its employ.

We will have to use force, because force is the only language our owners speak. They will use other dialects when possible, but sooner or later we will hear the accent of violence, the *lingua franca* of oppressors. Let us learn that now, before our Canadian independence movement has become a national liberation front. Today we get scraps from the table at the expense of our brothers in the less favoured colonies. Because the table is very big and the violence well organized, the scraps for the moment are more than enough to make many Canadians ignore the fact that they have been bought. But more of the players around the world are getting tired of the game; the U.S. gross national product may be at an all-time high, but it is also more dependent than ever on foreign markets and resources, the very areas the U.S. finds it hardest to control. Hence Vietnam, hence the Dominican Republic, hence military takeovers in Greece or Brazil. We of "the undefended border" are due for a steadily intensified relationship with our violent neighbour to the south.

And what will Canada do then, poor thing? First, she will have to recognize the validity of the Quebec nation's struggle for its independence. The French-speaking part of us will apparently, with the aid of one of the U.S.'s few competitors, be the first to break free. We must honour this struggle as one with our own, applaud and support it. We must not respond by wringing our hands and fearing our own absorption, our own reduction to a still lower status than that of our present pseudo-independence.

Rather, let us answer Quebec by developing our own equally strong struggle aimed at freeing Canada from U.S. domination by taking — and I say taking, not merely restricting or buying — our resources and industries out of U.S. hands. Let us advise the profiteers that the plunder called development is at an end. I say to people like George Grant, Farley Mowat, Alvin Hamilton, Walter Gordon, Tommy Douglas, James Minifie — whoever will stand for a genuinely free Canada — that we must all join in such a struggle, a Canadian independence movement. And if the New Left — or a new right or a new center for that matter — wants to join, then welcome. We must take Canada back, by whatever means our owner makes necessary, and then give the resources and industries of this land to its own people. Let us organize a new Canada in which people, not American-controlled corporations, come first.

Of course, what I am talking about is called the American Dream. It is the idea that this continent offers a fresh chance to develop a different kind of society, one free from the oppression inherited from the past. Once the United States was the locus of that dream — and men like Paine, Thoreau, and Whitman spoke for it. Today, the dream is fact in Havana, and people like the Latin American guerillas, the Québecois, and the black Americans are struggling to grasp it; the United States government and the military-business interests it represents have become the most effective enemies of the dream. But it is still fresh in Canada — we have the space, the people, and we could grasp the opportunity to make it real. And someday the 'mericans, especially the 'merican soldiers, will stop burning huts long enough to see it's what most of them want too.

As I Think of Where Today I Can Get th Rent Money

Bill Bissett

it becomes necessary
to speak in analogies.
There's two wars on,
both run by th U.S.,
one in Vietnam, th other
in Dominican Republic.

So what does that mean,
does it help to speak
this clearly, that you become
only anti-American; there's
trouble within th human
heart, where we move

toward each other, trusting,
there's trouble, the beat is
abridged, blink, we shut
out concern, love only

what we can abuse of this fellow
human we meet, whose address
is known to everyone, his number
filed within 30 seconds' reach, he is
our self with whom we don't join hands.

A Borderline Case

David Helwig

For a long time I was angry about the war in Vietnam. Now I think of it as hopeless. For several years I have thought that the Americans should not be there, not for the good of the country, not even for the good of the world. My demands are unreasonable. I think the Americans should get out. Altogether. They are interfering in a culture they don't belong to and don't understand. Defending Europe against Russia after 1945 was a policy that made sense because Europe and America had a lot in common; they were part of the same world, and the values defended were endemic and viable. To defend Africa against the Chinese may be a legitimate exercise of power on the grounds that the Chinese know no more of Africa than the Americans, and the African countries may need time to try out their new nations before committing them. But to defend Vietnam against the Vietnamese is an exercise in pointlessness.

So there I am; I have a position on the biggest fact of American political life.

And less than an hour's drive away, just out of sight, is a northern corner of the United States. It's been that way most of the time since I was ten. When I was a kid, I could walk two blocks, look across a mile of river, and see the U.S. The American Coast Guard Station was at the edge of the water, and at the old fort above, I could see the red and black storm warnings. Now and then on an American holiday, we would cross the river and see a parade. The way the American soldiers marched was comical. They didn't lift their feet or swing their arms the way we'd been taught in the cadet corps at school. I suppose all the Americans in Vietnam march in the same comic way if they march at all.

For several years, the Niagara River was all that separated me from the Americans. We knew all about them, of course, that they were mouthy, rude, and not much as soldiers (everyone had Second World War stories to prove this). But in New York State you could see movies on Sunday, and every now and then, we did. We might even smuggle back a bit of something. I remember my grandfather, an argumentative Yorkshireman who claimed that the capitalists would call him a communist and that the Bolsheviks would call him a capitalist (and was probably right on both counts), once got involved in a fierce dispute about whether it was legal to bring back an open package of cigarettes.

It's just as well the American immigration officials didn't ask him what kind of political opinions he was bringing into their country, or we might have missed our movie.

Then, before long, I was eighteen, or thought I looked it, and you could drink beer in New York State at eighteen. We would go across after it was too dark to play golf to eat pizza and drink American beer — Miller's High Life — and a pretty high old life it was, between Korea and Vietnam, and you didn't get drafted in Canada anyway.

Over these years, I met a lot of Americans, those I met on trips across the river and the rich ones from Buffalo who spent the summer in town. Then I went away to school and met Henry. From Brooklyn. He was not exactly a patriot, was thankful that his draft status was low, but got irritated enough at complacent remarks about the superiority of Canadian education that now and then he made me realize that I was a foreigner on this continent too.

Once I went to visit him in Brooklyn, to spend a few days, not just a few hours, in the States. Just before the train got to New York, it went underground. When I phoned Henry from the station, there was some confusion about directions, and I didn't see the sky again for about three hours. I wandered underground through unknown subway stations asking questions, but people either refused to answer (afraid of being mugged maybe?) or said, pretty rudely, that they didn't know anything about it. I'm glad I wasn't in real trouble.

I haven't heard from Henry for a couple of years or so. As far as I know he's living in California married to a Quaker . . .

but then a man who claimed he could fart the Star-Spangled Banner might end up anywhere.

So I've known Americans, even though I can't make much connection between the ones I've known and the acts of their government. Of course, I always have that trouble with politics; I can seldom relate the events of the big world to the people I know.

Aside from all this, the U.S.A. means TV. Since the '40's I have never been out of range of American television except for a couple of years I spent in England (and even there my wife and I would go downstairs every Saturday night to watch Perry Mason with our senile landlady). From Steve Allen and *Father Knows Best* to Johnny Carson and *Get Smart*, I've watched them all. That archetypal American, Richard Kimble, always got to me as he slouched along, innocent and misunderstood. I suppose Lyndon Johnson thinks of himself as a man like Richard Kimble, making painful decisions, blamed wrongly, a good man at heart.

Hey, hey, LBJ, how many kids have you killed today?

* * *

When Kennedy was killed, I felt as though I had lost someone.

And watching a freedom march, while Joan Baez and others sang "We Shall Overcome," I tried to explain to my young daughter what it was all about and found I couldn't talk right.

* * *

One spring when I was about eighteen, the ice jammed at the mouth of the Niagara River. It jammed solid, heaped and bulged, strong enough to walk on. I started across one Sunday afternoon, just for the hell of it; I knew I wouldn't be allowed to go ashore on the other side. When I got about halfway, my nose started to bleed for some unknown reason, and I had to turn back. Within a day or so the ice had cleared away, and there was no longer any chance to walk there. I couldn't have gone ashore anyway.

My Thoughts on Americans and the U.S.A.

Desmond Pacey

My thoughts on Americans and the U.S.A. depend upon the particular hat I am wearing when the thoughts occur.

As a citizen of the world, I fear the self-righteous precipitancy of this most powerful single country, which goes rushing into places like Vietnam with generally good motives but with most dangerous effects. I calm my fears somewhat, however, by reminding myself that the most intelligent and damning criticism of such actions and policies comes from within the United States itself and that the union is far from being monolithic. General Westmoreland found much more powerful critics in John Kenneth Galbraith and Robert Kennedy than he is likely to find in me.

As a citizen of Canada, I resent the economic and cultural pressure of the United States upon us, while granting again that it is not the result of conscious malevolence on its part but an inevitable by-product of propinquity and disproportion. Moreover, I think that Canadians are themselves largely to blame for permitting this pressure to be so effective. We are slow to invest in our own resources and then reproach Americans for doing so; we are halfhearted in our support of Canadian magazines, films, painting, music, and literature and then have the nerve to complain that we are swamped by American products; we reproach Americans for taking little interest in our poets and novelists, but we take little interest in them ourselves. I should like to see a much more positive Canadianism as an antidote to the Americanization of Canada. Moreover, we tend to import the worst of contemporary American culture and to ignore the best. The American television programs, for example, that are brought to Canada by the C.B.C. are monstrosities such as *Dundee and the Culhanes*,

Green Acres, and *Bonanza,* whereas the many fine plays and interviews that are shown on the National Educational network and even on some of the commercial networks are available only to those who can afford cable TV or have the good luck to live close to the border.

As a Canadian professor I am envious of the great libraries and other academic resources of the leading American universities such as Harvard, Yale, and California and at the same time patriotically contemptuous of the low standards of the weaker American universities and colleges. In this dual reaction of mixed envy and contempt, I am probably typical of Canadian academics; I hope I am typical also in my determination to do what I can to build up our own resources to the point where we shall not need to be defensive. The neglect of Canadian university libraries over the first hundred years of our history is nothing short of a national disgrace.

As a private person with strong literary interests I have nothing but admiration for American literature. The rambling essays and quaint tales of Washington Irving have always intrigued me; Emerson and Thoreau are writers whose thoughts have influenced my own thinking more perhaps than any other writers in English; Melville, Whitman, and Jeffers impress me by their symbolic power, their moral profundity, and their refusal to compromise; Henry James I regard as the most subtle and skillful psychological novelist I have ever read; Ernest Hemingway, William Faulkner, and Thomas Wolfe were the heroes of my adolescence, and I still read them with deep enjoyment. What is significant about this highly selective and incomplete list of my American literary favourites is that all the authors named were fierce or subtle critics of what is often assumed to be the real America — the America of material wealth and power, of conformity, of dollar-drunkenness and gadget-madness. For example, the quotations from Emerson and Thoreau that have become part of my mental stock-in-trade are my chief ammunition against materialism and conformity — "Whosoever would be a man must be a non-conformist"; "Things are in the saddle and ride mankind"; "Let the single man plant himself indomitably on his instincts and there abide, and the whole world will come round to him"; "Never forget that a pop-gun is always and only a pop-gun though the ancient and honourable of the earth declare it to be the crack of doom."

All of which brings me to my main point — that the redeeming feature of Americans is their capacity for self-criticism. Since they are so good at self-criticism, they do not need much help from Canadians — we should be much more usefully employed in criticizing ourselves. Canadians, it seems to me, are at least as open to criticism as Americans in almost every respect, and yet how seldom do we subject ourselves to searching self-examination? We criticize the Americans for their involvement in Vietnam — but usually ignore the fact that we are benefiting from their involvement by selling them arms and military supplies. We jeer at the Americans for their racial problem and blithely ignore the discrimination that exists in our own midst. We bemoan our dependence upon American culture but do almost nothing to support the emergence of an endemic Canadian culture. We criticize American preoccupation with money and things — and at the same time clamour for parity of wage-rates and salary-scales and for an equal standard of living. It is difficult to resist the conclusion that there is a large measure of hypocrisy in the Canadian attitude to the U.S.A.

Oh Canada

John Robert Colombo

Canada could have enjoyed:
    English government,
        French culture,
            and American know-how.

Instead it ended up with:
    English know-how,
        French government,
            and American culture.

Enlightened (?) Self-Interest of the U.S.

C. W. Gonick

The conventional Canadian response to domestic stagnation and economic depression has been the urge to establish some new commercial alignment with the United States. Historically, the continentalist impulse has taken the form of reciprocity, free trade, or common markets. Only when such proposals have been rejected by the U.S., thereby precluding dramatic external commercial expansion, has the government of Canada opted for internal economic expansion and structural change as an alternative policy. Macdonald's celebrated "National Policy," for example — Confederation, the opening up of the West, the building of the Trans-Canadian railway system, and the imposition of protective tariffs — was brought into effect only after the Canadian provinces had been cut off from the British imperial system and only after they had been spurned by the Americans in their bid for a renewal of the reciprocity treaty.

Under the umbrella of high tariffs, however, a new version of continentalism was emerging — the branch plant economy. In order to supply the growing Canadian market for consumer goods, American manufacturers have been forced to establish branch plants on this side of the border. Indeed, the attraction of American capital was one of the main reasons originally offered for erecting tariff barriers. In addition, great American resource-based corporations nearly a century ago began to exploit Canadian forests and minerals to supply the industrial mills of the United States. The result has been pervasive American ownership of Canadian industry and the near American monopolization of Canadian trade. American corporations control ninety-one per cent of the Canadian rubber industry, thirty-five per cent of the pulp and paper industry, fifty-two per cent of the agricultural machinery industry, ninety-seven per cent of the automobile and parts industry, sixty-six per cent of the electrical apparatus industry, fifty-four per cent of chemicals, sixty per cent of petroleum and natural gas, and over fifty per cent of the mining industry; between a quarter and a third of the goods produced in Canada are exported to the U.S.; in all, seventy per cent of all Canadian exports are sent to the United States while sixty per cent of our imports come from the United States.

Largely as a consequence of the branch plant system, Canadian manufacturing industries have productivity levels which are, on the average, one third lower than their counterparts in the United States. This has meant lower wages, higher prices, and a standard of living that is no more than three quarters that of the United States. One of the major reasons for this persistently lower level of productivity is that the branch plant is restricted to producing for the Canadian market and that, trying to produce all the myriads of models and designs that the parent company produces with its several plants within the U.S.A., it is unable to gain all the efficiencies that ordinarily go with bigness. The other major reason is the lower educational levels and skills of the Canadian labour force. This is the lesson reiterated over and over again by the Economic Council of Canada, and its conclusion is clear: invest more funds in human capital and, within a framework of freer trade, engage in greater specialization.

A number of prominent economists have joined in on the chorus, but they carry the argument further. They claim that the general movement towards freer world trade is dimming, that the world is dividing into regional trading blocs, and that if Canada is to gain access to larger markets it will have to be the U.S. market by means of a free trade agreement between the two countries. (With some justification, they would also argue that the tariff reductions brought about throughout the Western world via the Kennedy Round will serve to strengthen the trade ties between Canada and the U.S. rather than facilitate the development of European markets for Canadian goods.) This has long been the view of the powerful Canadian-American Committee, and it was also echoed at the Liberal

Party policy conference held in the spring of 1967. The conference went so far as to pass a resolution advocating just such a proposal. There is, as we have seen, nothing new in this agitation. It is a revival of the century-old panacea of economic integration with the U.S.

Indeed, it can scarcely be denied that Canada is already a satellite, regional economy of the U.S. The function of Canada as a region within the continental North American economy is to supply staple commodities as substitutes for the increasingly depleted resources of the United States. American corporate ownership in Canada generates and perpetuates this branch plant economy: Americans develop our resource industries in order to supply U.S. industry with raw materials; Americans develop our manufacturing industries to supply our limited domestic market. Markets for our resources outside the U.S. are unexplored; foreign markets for our manufactured goods are untapped.

Because Canada has become a satellite state, the Canadian government lacks the leverage to direct the economy along a path divergent from that of the U.S.; for example, the Canadian economy cannot evade a depression emanating from the U.S., and the dose of inflation we are experiencing at the present time is brought about by the excessive continental-wide demand for resources generated by the Vietnam War. In this context the function of the Canadian government has been to adjust to changes occurring in the U.S. as smoothly and efficiently as possible and to introduce measures which parallel the policy initiatives of Washington.

We hear much critical comment from the economic nationalists on the economic costs of our satellite status. Undoubtedly a strong economic case can be made for a more independent Canada, and I have been one, among others, who made it. Here the argument is not in any way anti-American. It is an argument against a predominant Canadian economic dependence upon any other single national economy. Our economy is today overwhelmingly tied to the economy of the United States, and that is why attention is focused upon Canadian-U.S. relations. The same arguments would hold if the nation were rather Japan, the U.K., France, or the U.S.S.R.

My own opposition to continentalism rests, however, primarily on moral grounds. The British historian Arnold Toynbee has said of America, ". . . (she) is no longer the inspirer and leader of the World Revolution . . . (but the) leader of a world-wide anti-revolutionary movement of vested interests. She now stands for what Rome stood for." Indeed, if Vietnam has not taught us this lesson, then it has taught us nothing. Vietnam is not an aberration. It is not a mistake as the liberal opposition to the war contends. There have already been many Vietnams — in Greece, in Iran, in Guatemala, in Cuba, in Santo Domingo — and there will be many more Vietnams. The American counter-revolutionary posture may be an inevitable result of her economic system, or it may be based on other factors. As has been suggested by the American historian William A. Williams, the Americans may simply be following their traditional bent of evading domestic economic and social crises by turning outward. In the face of domestic social problems that have now taken on critical proportions, the Americans are busy conquering outer space, penetrating new European markets, and policing their empire in Asia and Latin America. The "great evasion" Williams talks of is "the manipulation of nature to avoid a confrontation with the human conditions and with the challenge of building a true community." Alternatively, the American counter-revolutionary position may be the result of a religious hang-up. Robert Heilbroner, for example, argues that "it is . . . the fear of losing our place in the sun . . . that motivates a great deal of anti-communism on which so much of American foreign policy seems to be founded . . . . The rise of communism (in the underdeveloped world) would signal the end of capitalism as the dominant world order and would force the acknowledgement that America no longer constituted the model on which the future of world civilization would be mainly based . . . . The existence of communism frightens American capitalism as the rise of Protestantism frightened the Catholic Church or the French Revolution, the English aristocracy."

Whichever factor is primary, ideological or economic, the Americans are bent on policing the world to ensure that challenges to their system are restricted, isolated, and defeated. The fact that the American system is unworkable in the underdeveloped world, that only a collectivist-type solution can vault these backward countries into the literate and in-dustrial society of the twentieth century, is irrelevant to the Americans. They are going to protect their empire, "retain these countries for the free world," even if it means destroying them and obliterating their people. The policy option left to the Americans in Vietnam is now withdrawal or genocide. And there is no indication that the first option is acceptable to the high command. Nor can a war of such brutal dimensions fail to have a brutalizing impact within the United States itself. As the war has escalated and its futility and immorality have become increasingly evident, the voices of dissent have inevitably multiplied, and civil disobedience has taken on serious proportions. It is no surpise, then, that the days of the witch hunts have returned. Investigation, arrests, censorship, and White House intimidation are placing the right of free speech in serious jeopardy. More generally, Mary McCarthy writes of the "uselessness of our free institutions . . . to inter-pose any check on a war of this character, opposed by most so-called thinking persons." She concludes, rightly in my view, that this suggests that "freedom in the United States is no longer a political value and is seen simply as the right to self-expression, as in the dance, psychodrama, be-ins, kinky sex, baking ceramics."

The struggle against the free traders and others of their ilk is important, in my view, because continentalism makes us accomplices to American interventionism, sucks us into the American system, saps our will to be different. Is there a viable economic alternative to continentalism? There is no question in my mind that there is. There are vast markets in Europe and Asia, unavailable to the Canadian economy only because of American laws and the trading policies of Ameri-can parent companies. A fully employed Canadian economy, moreover, is now in a position to generate enough savings to satisfy most of our capital needs. The problem is that a sig-nificant part of these savings are American controlled: a large portion of so-called foreign investment is really Canadian savings taking the form of profits earned in American branch plants and reinvested. Actually, American branch plants ex-port more capital to the parent companies than they import from them. In the area of direct capital, then, Canada is a net exporter to the U.S. rather than vice versa. With respect to both trade and capital, then, our ties to the American economy rest upon the continuation of the branch plant system. If we are to develop new markets and gain ownership and control over our savings, if, in other words, we are to break out of the continentalist structure, we must break up the branch plant system. This means greatly restricting the position of American capital in the Canadian economy. It also means withdrawal from NATO and NORAD and at last conducting an independent foreign policy.

Biographies

MARGARET ATWOOD's *The Circle Game*, 1966, won the Governor General's Award for poetry in Canada. She recently taught in Montreal and now lives in Edmonton. Her most recent book is *The Animals in That Country*.

HENRY BEISSEL is a poet, editor of *Edge Magazine* in Montreal, and an associate professor of English at Sir George Williams University. His book of poems, *New Wings for Icarus*, was published in 1967.

EARLE BIRNEY has been called "the dean of Canadian poets." He is the author of two novels, *Turvey*, 1949, and *Down the Long Table*, 1955. He has twice won the Governor General's Award for poetry. Birney's *Selected Poems* was published in 1967. He was recently Centennial-Writer-in-Residence at Waterloo University and now teaches at the University of California at Irvine.

BILL BISSETT is a young Vancouver poet. His current book is *Lebanon Voices* published last year.

GEORGE BOWERING is a poet, novelist, critic, assistant professor, and Writer-in-Residence at Sir George Williams University. He has published three books of poetry and a novel, *Mirror on the Floor*, 1967.

J. M. S. CARELESS is with the Department of History at the University of Toronto. He has received a Carnegie Award (1958), the Tyrrell Medal (1962), the University of British

Columbia's Medal for popular biography, and several fellow-ships. He has twice won the Governor General's Award. His current book is *The Union of the Canadas*.

JOHN ROBERT COLOMBO is an editor of one of Canada's foremost literary magazines, *The Tamarack Review*. He has published three books of poetry, the last entitled *Abracadabra*.

LOUIS DUDEK is a poet, university instructor, critic, editor, and general man-of-letters. He has published many books of poetry. With Michael Gnarowski, he edited *The Making of Modern Poetry in Canada*, published in 1967.

ARNOLD EDINBOROUGH is president of Saturday Night Publications. His book *Canada* appeared in 1962, and he also contributed to *Mass Media in Canada* and *The Restless Church*.

ROBERT FULFORD is one of Canada's finest literary journalists. His book *This Was Expo* was published earlier this year. Mr. Fulford is now editor of *Saturday Night* magazine.

HUGH GARNER is a novelist, short story writer, essayist, and journalist. He won the Governor General's Award for *Hugh Garner's Best Stories*, 1963. His most recent book, *Men and Women*, appeared in 1966.

DAVE GODFREY is a short story writer and editor of the experimental publishing venture, House of Anansi. His selected stories, *Death Goes Better with Coca-Cola*, was published in 1967. A year ago he won two President's Medals of the University of Western Ontario for the best short story and best essay published in Canada.

C. W. GONICK, editor of the magazine *Canadian Dimension*, is with the Department of Political Science at the University of Manitoba. He is a strong advocate of a more independent Canada and has recently initiated the formation of a society to work towards this goal.

GEORGE GRANT is chairman in the Department of Religion at McMaster University. He wrote the controversial *Lament for a Nation,* dealing with Canada's eventual disappearance as a nation.

DAVID HELWIG is a poet and playwright who teaches at Queen's University. A book of his poetry and plays, *Figures in a Landscape,* was published in 1968.

GEORGE JONAS is an editor for the Canadian Broadcasting Corporation's script department in Toronto. His book of poems is *The Absolute Smile,* 1967.

NAIM KATTAN is in charge of the literary section of the Canada Council. For two years he was an editor for the Laurendeau-Dunton Commission, and in 1962-63 he lectured in the Social Sciences at Laval University. Mr. Kattan serves on the editorial board of *Les Lettres Nouvelles* (Paris) and is a frequent contributor to literary magazines.

LIONEL KEARNS teaches English at Simon Fraser University. His current book of poetry is *Pointing,* which appeared in 1967.

WILLIAM KILBOURN is chairman of the Department of Humanities at York University. He has written *The Elements Combined,* *The Firebrand,* and *The Making of the Nation.* *The Firebrand,* a biography of William Lyon Mackenzie, won two national awards for biography and literature.

LAURIER LAPIERRE is director of the French Canada Studies Program at McGill University and was the New Democratic Party candidate for the federal constituency of Lachine. He was also associated with the late lamented television program *This Hour Has Seven Days.* He wrote *Genesis of a Nation* and has three more books in preparation.

MARGARET LAURENCE is a novelist and short story writer. Her novel *A Jest of God* won the Governor General's Award for fiction and has been made into a film. Her first novel, *The Stone Angel,* has been published in the United States and England as well as in Canada.

IRVING LAYTON has written and edited some twenty books. His selected poems, *A Red Carpet for the Sun*, 1959, won the Governor General's Award for poetry. His latest book is *The Shattered Plinths*.

DENNIS LEE teaches at Rochdale College in Toronto. His recent book of poems is *The Kingdom of Absence*.

DOROTHY LIVESAY has published many books of poetry, her latest being *The Unquiet Bed*, which appeared in 1967. She has twice won the Governor General's Award for poetry and was Poet-in-Residence at the University of New Brunswick. She now teaches at the University of Alberta in Edmonton.

BARRY LORD is a poet and artist. He has published one book of poems. Until recently he edited the magazine *Canadian Art*, but he now teaches communications at Conestoga College in Kitchener.

JACK LUDWIG is a novelist, short story writer, and university instructor. He has lived much of his adult life in the U.S. His novel *Confusions* was the subject of much comment, and his new novel, *Above Ground*, was published earlier this year. This year he is Writer-in-Residence at the University of Toronto.

EDWARD MCCOURT is a prolific writer of both fiction and biography with a long series of novels set in the Canadian West to his credit. He is currently teaching with the Department of English at the University of Saskatchewan. His most recent book, *Saskatchewan*, was published earlier this year.

ANDRE MAJOR is a young Quebec poet with a separatist outlook. His first two books were *Le froid se meurt* and *Holocauste à deux voix*, both published in 1961.

TOM MARSHALL is a young poet and English instructor at Queen's University. A book of his poetry is scheduled for publication in 1968.

ROBIN MATHEWS is a young poet formerly with the Department of English at the University of Alberta. He has published two books of poetry and written numerous articles on Canadian subjects. He presently lives in Paris, France.

JAMES M. MINIFIE was chief of the Canadian Broadcasting Corporation's Washington news bureau. His books include *Peace-Maker or Powder Monkey* and *Open at the Top*. His latest book is *Who's Your Fat Friend?*, which appeared in 1967.

FARLEY MOWAT is a prolific author and broadcaster. Of his numerous books, *Westviking*, 1965, dealing with the ancient Norse in Greenland and North America, is perhaps the best known. Other successes have been *The Dog Who Wouldn't Be*, *Never Cry Wolf*, *The Desperate People*, *People of the Deer*, and *Polar Passion*, to name a few.

JOHN NEWLOVE is a "professional" poet. He has lived in the prairie provinces, Vancouver, and Halifax. His best book is *Moving in Alone*, 1965. His most recent is a book of poems entitled *Black Night Window*.

C. J. NEWMAN is a Montreal poet and novelist. His novel *We Always Take Care of Our Own* was published in 1965.

PETER C. NEWMAN is one of Canada's best known and most respected political journalists. His books are *Flame of Power* and later *Renegade in Power*, a best-selling biography of John Diefenbaker.

ERIC NICOL, one of Canada's most popular writers, is a columnist for *The Vancouver Province*. His books have won several prizes, including the Leacock Medal for humour.

ALDEN NOWLAN has written short stories as well as several books of poetry. His latest book is *Bread, Wine and Salt*, 1967, which won the Governor General's Award for poetry, 1967. He has received a Guggenheim Fellowship for poetry.

MICHAEL ONDAATJE was born in Ceylon and educated in Canada. His book of poems, *The Dainty Monsters*, appeared in 1967.

DESMOND PACEY is a short story writer, critic, and now Dean of Graduate Studies at the University of New Brunswick. Two of his books are *The Picnic* (short stories) and *Creative Writing in Canada*.

A. W. PURDY is a well-known Canadian poet. He received the Governor General's Award for *The Cariboo Horses*, which appeared in 1965. His two most recent books are *Poems for All the Annettes* and *Wild Grape Vine*, both published in 1968.

MORDECAI RICHLER is one of Canada's best known and best novelists. He has written screen plays, articles, and many short stories. His novel *The Apprenticeship of Duddy Kravitz*, 1959, received praise both in Canada and elsewhere. His new novel, *Cocksure*, has been widely acclaimed by enthusiastic reviews. This year he is Writer-in-Residence at Sir George Williams University.

RAY SMITH was born in Cape Breton, Nova Scotia—as might be expected. "Cape Breton Is the Thought Control Center of Canada" is his first published story, but he has since had another accepted for publication by *Prism International*.

RAYMOND SOUSTER has published so many books of poetry it is likely that he has lost count of the exact number. His collected poetry, *The Colour of the Times*, 1964, won the Governor General's Award for poetry. His current book, *As Is*, was published in 1967. He has also edited poetry magazines and was co-editor of Contact Press.

PETER STEVENS is with the Department of English at the University of Saskatchewan. A book of his poetry will be published in 1968.

STEPHEN VIZINCZEY by-passed commercial publishers three years ago, publishing his own book *In Praise of Older Women*. The book sold extremely well and attracted favourable critical comment. Mr. Vizinczey is now writing in England.

JOHN W. WARNOCK is an assistant professor of political science at the University of Saskatchewan. He has written *An Analytical Study of Canadian Defense Policy Since World War II* (not yet published). Born in the United States, he has lived in Canada since 1963.

PHYLLIS WEBB is a program organizer with the Canadian Broadcasting Corporation. Her last two books are *The Sea Is Also a Garden*, 1962, and *Naked Poems*, 1965.

GEORGE WOODCOCK is a man-of-letters in the twentieth century sense. He edits the magazine *Canadian Literature* and has written many books. *The Crystal Spirit*, 1967, his study of George Orwell, won the Governor General's Award for non-fiction.

LARRY ZOLF is a producer-reporter-interviewer for *The Public Eye* and a frequent contributor to weekly radio programs. In 1965, he was awarded the CBC's Wilderness Award for the best television journalism of the year for the film *Strike— Man Against Computers*.